Collins

PRACTICE MULTIPLE CHOICE QUESTIONS

CAPE®
Accounting

Carl Herrera
Lystra Stephens-James

Collins

HarperCollins Publishers Ltd
The News Building
1 London Bridge Street
London SE1 9GF

First edition 2017

10 9 8 7 6 5 4 3 2

ISBN 978-0-00-822203-1

www.collins.co.uk/caribbeanschools

A catalogue record for this book is available from the British Library.

Typeset by QBS Learning
Printed and bound by CPI Group (UK) Ltd, Croydon, CR0 4YY

Author: Carl Herrera and Lystra Stephens-James
Publisher: Elaine Higgleton
Commissioning Editor: Ben Gardiner
Managing Editor: Sarah Thomas
Project Manager: Alissa McWhinnie
Copy Editor: Stephen Cashmore
Proofreader: Alta Bridges
Answer checker: Kay Hawkins
Artwork: QBS Learning
Cover design: Kevin Robbins and Gordon MacGilp
Production: Lauren Crisp

Contents

Download answers for free at www.collins.co.uk/caribbeanschools

Structure of the CAPE® Accounting Paper 1 Examination

There are **45 questions** in the **Unit 1** examination; and **45 questions** in the **Unit 2** examination. The duration of each examination is **1½ hours**. The papers are worth **40%** of your final examination mark.

The Paper 1 examinations test the following core areas of the syllabus.

Unit 1: Financial Accounting

Section	Number of Questions
Module 1: Accounting, Theory, Recording and Control Systems	90
Module 2: Preparation of Financial Statements	95
Module 3: Financial Reporting and Interpretation	70
Total	**255**

Unit 2: Cost and Management Accounting

Section	Number of Questions
Module 1: Costing Principles	75
Module 2: Costing Systems	80
Module 3: Planning and Decision Making	85
Total	**240**

The questions test two profiles, **knowledge and comprehension**, and **use of knowledge**. Questions will be presented in a variety of ways including the use of figures, data and graphs.

Each question is allocated 1 mark. You will <u>not</u> lose a mark if a question is answered incorrectly.

Examination Tips

General strategies for answering multiple choice questions:

- Read every word of each question very carefully and make sure you understand exactly what it is asking. Even if you think that the question appears simple or straightforward there may be important information you could easily omit, especially small, but very important words such as *all* or *only*.

- When faced with a question that seems unfamiliar, re-read it very carefully. Underline or circle the key pieces of information provided. Re-read it again if necessary to make sure you are very clear as to what it is asking and that you are not misinterpreting it.

- Each question has four options, **A**, **B**, **C** and **D**, and only one is the correct answer. Look at all the options very carefully as the differences between them may be very subtle; never just stop when you come across an option you think is the one required. Cross out options that you know are incorrect for certain. There may be two options that appear very similar; identify the difference between the two so you can select the correct answer.

- You have approximately 2 minutes per question. Some questions can be answered in less than 1 minute while other questions may require longer because of the reasoning or calculation involved. Do not spend too long on any one question.

- If a question appears difficult place a mark, such as an asterisk, on your answer sheet alongside the question number, to remind yourself to return to it when you have finished answering all the other questions. Remember to carefully remove the asterisk, or other markings, from the answer sheet using a good clean eraser as soon as you have completed the question.

- Answer every question. Marks are not deducted for incorrect answers. Therefore it is in your best interest to make an educated guess in instances where you do not know the answer. Never leave a question unanswered.

- Always ensure that you are shading the correct question number on your answer sheet. It is very easy to make a mistake, especially if you plan on returning to skipped questions.

- Some questions may ask which of the options is NOT correct or is INCORRECT. Pay close attention to this because it is easy to fail to see the words *NOT* or *INCORRECT* and answer the question incorrectly.

- Some questions may give two or more answers that could be correct and you are asked to determine which is the *BEST* or *MOST LIKELY*. You must consider each answer very carefully before making your choice because the differences between them may be very subtle.

- When a question gives three or four answers numbered **I, II** and **III** or **I, II, III** and **IV**, one or more of these answers may be correct. You will then be given four combinations as options, for example:

  (A) I only
  (B) I and II only
  (C) II and III only
  (D) I, II and III

  Place a tick by all the answers that you think are correct before you decide on the final correct combination.

- Do not make any assumptions about your choice of options, just because two answers in succession have been C, it does not mean that the next one cannot be C as well.

- Try to leave time at the end of the examination to check over your answers, but never change an answer until you have thought about it again very carefully.

Strategies for the CAPE® Accounting Paper 1

- A silent, non-programmable calculator is allowed in the examination. You are required to provide your own calculator. Since different brands of calculators have different features it is advisable to take a calculator you are familiar with.

- You may be required to do simple calculations in the Paper 1 examinations. Be very careful and accurate when performing calculations. It is very easy to make an error and there may be an incorrect option similar to your calculation. For questions requiring you to perform a calculation, work out the answer before you look at the four options. Do this by writing your working on the question paper. If you do not find your answer in the options, you can then go back and recheck your working for mistakes.

- Some questions are accompanied by figures, graphs, tables or prose. Read and inspect these carefully and use them to derive the best option for the question. You may make your own sketches to help you answer the questions.

Unit 1: Financial Accounting

Nature and scope of financial accounting

1 Financial accounting is best defined as

(A) recording economic events of entities   (A)

(B) examining future events for economic decisions   (B)

(C) generally accepted accounting principles of a country   (C)

(D) recording, summarising and communicating economic events of entities.   (D)

Limitations

2 Though financial statements are useful, they are limited because

(A) reports are based on current market value   (A)

(B) they do not use estimates   (B)

(C) non-financial success factors cannot be measured and reported monetarily   (C)

(D) there are no standards for reporting the economic events of a business.   (D)

Users

3 Which user is matched correctly with its major need?

User	Major Need	
(A) Shareholders	Assess managers' stewardship	(A)
(B) Trade union	Potential equity investment	(B)
(C) Government	Analyse company's performance in relation to others	(C)
(D) Trade creditors	Assess securities to provide loans	(D)

4 Which user has the need of financial reporting to assess the company's ability to pay its employees increased salaries?

(A) Government   (A)

(B) Trade unions   (B)

(C) Trade creditors   (C)

(D) Shareholders   (D)

The accounting cycle

Figure 1.1 refers to <u>items 5–7</u>.

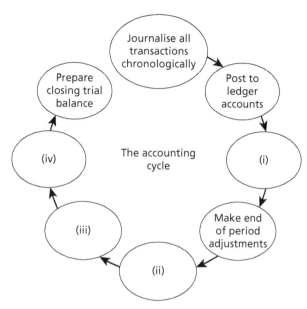

Figure 1.1

5 In Figure 1.1 above (i) represents

    (A) journalising closing entries   Ⓐ

    (B) preparing an adjusted trial balance   Ⓑ

    (C) preparing a trial balance   Ⓒ

    (D) preparing financial statements.   Ⓓ

6 In Figure 1.1 above (ii) represents

    (A) journalising closing entries   Ⓐ

    (B) preparing an adjusted trial balance   Ⓑ

    (C) preparing a trial balance   Ⓒ

    (D) preparing financial statements.   Ⓓ

7 In Figure 1.1 above (iii) represents

    (A) journalising closing entries   Ⓐ

    (B) preparing an adjusted trial balance   Ⓑ

    (C) preparing a trial balance   Ⓒ

    (D) preparing financial statements.   Ⓓ

8 Which basis of accounting is required for the preparation of general purpose financial statements?

(A) Cash basis   Ⓐ

(B) Accrual basis   Ⓑ

(C) Depreciation basis   Ⓒ

(D) LIFO basis   Ⓓ

9 Which of the following groups are represented on the IASB?

    I Academia

    II Auditing professionals

    III Users of financial statements

(A) I and II   Ⓐ

(B) I and III   Ⓑ

(C) II and III   Ⓒ

(D) I, II and III   Ⓓ

10 Which steps are included in "Due Process"?

    I Steering Committee appointed by the IASB

    II Steering Committee collects IASs and IFRSs for the IASB

    III The Steering Committee prepares and presents a Point Outline to the IASB

(A) I and II   Ⓐ

(B) I and III   Ⓑ

(C) II and III   Ⓒ

(D) I, II and III   Ⓓ

11 Which Institute of Chartered Accountants belong to ICAC?

(A) Institute of Chartered Accountants of Cuba   Ⓐ

(B) Bahamas Institute of Chartered Accountants   Ⓑ

(C) Dominican Republic Institute of Chartered Accountants   Ⓒ

(D) Institute of Chartered Accountants of French Guyana   Ⓓ

12 Which are the reasons for adopting the IFRS for SMEs?

    I It makes it simpler for SMEs to comply.

    II It means that all businesses can have consistent reporting.

    III It reduces the cost associated with meeting the requirements of IASs and IFRSs.

(A) I and II   Ⓐ

(B) I and III   Ⓑ

(C) II and III   Ⓒ

(D) I, II and III   Ⓓ

Conceptual Framework of Accounting

13 Which of the following statements are included in the purposes of the Conceptual Framework of Accounting?

    I Promote harmonisation of regulations, accounting standards and procedures.

    II Assist auditors in forming an opinion to whether financial statements conform to IASs.

    III Provide information about the enterprise's resources, claims on resources and use of resources.

(A) I and II   Ⓐ

(B) I and III   Ⓑ

(C) II and III   Ⓒ

(D) I, II and III   Ⓓ

14 In Level 1 of the Conceptual Framework of Accounting, the objectives for including information in the financial statements is considered useful only if it is

(A) useful or helpful in assessing future cashflows (A)

(B) recorded on a cash basis (B)

(C) recording all assets at fair market rake each year (C)

(D) assisting the IASB in developing future standards. (D)

15 The headquarters of ICAC is located in

(A) Jamaica (A)

(B) Barbados (B)

(C) Grenada (C)

(D) Trinidad and Tobago. (D)

16 The second level of the Conceptual Framework of Accounting consists of

I elements of financial statements

II purposes of financial information

III characteristics of financial information.

(A) I and II (A)

(B) I and III (B)

(C) II and III (C)

(D) I, II and III (D)

Elements of the financial statements

17 Dividends due to shareholders is listed as what element of the financial statements?

(A) Comprehensive income (A)

(B) Investment by owners (B)

(C) Distribution to owners (C)

(D) Revenue (D)

18 Organisation costs belong to what category of elements of the financial statement?

(A) Assets   (A)

(B) Liabilities   (B)

(C) Revenue   (C)

(D) Expenses   (D)

19 Treasury stock belongs to what category of the element of the financial statements?

(A) Distribution to owners   (A)

(B) Investment by owners   (B)

(C) Equity   (C)

(D) Expenses   (D)

Qualitative characteristics

20 Naparima Communications, an agent for YouCall cell phones, receives 12% commission on the sale of each YouCall cell phone. Naparima Communications records the sale of each cell phone as revenue and the payment of the 88% to YouCall as expenses. Qualitatively, this means the accounting information

(A) is not reliable   (A)

(B) provides irrelevant information   (B)

(C) breaches substance over form   (C)

(D) lacks consistency.   (D)

21 The statement, "Financial reporting provided for users must not be so complex that a user with a reasonable knowledge of business and economic activities and accounting, with a willingness to study the information with reasonable diligence, can comprehend it" follows the Conceptual Framework of Accounting's qualitative characteristics of

(A) comparability   (A)

(B) understandability   (B)

(C) consistency   (C)

(D) substance over form.   (D)

22 For accounting information to be relevant according to the Conceptual Framework of Accounting it must

    I possess predictive value

    II be complete

    III be timely.

(A) I and II   Ⓐ

(B) I and III   Ⓑ

(C) II and III   Ⓒ

(D) I, II and III   Ⓓ

23 A manufacturing company has difficulty with its cashflow. As a result, it sold its machinery to a similar company and gets them back by a lease. The accounting information should be recorded in accordance with

(A) understandability   Ⓐ

(B) substance over form   Ⓑ

(C) consistency   Ⓒ

(D) comparability.   Ⓓ

24 When a business applies the same accounting policy to similar items in the accounting period and from one period to the next it follows the

(A) consistency concept   Ⓐ

(B) comparability principle   Ⓑ

(C) substance over form principle   Ⓒ

(D) prudence concept.   Ⓓ

Accounting principles, concepts and conventions

25 The accounting concept that assumes that the business shall continue for the foreseeable future and as a result the financial statements are prepared considering the organisation's continuance is called

(A) historic cost   Ⓐ

(B) revenue recognition   Ⓑ

(C) materiality   Ⓒ

(D) going concern.   Ⓓ

26 Caribbean Insurance Company has its headquarters in St Kitts and branches in Belize and Barbados. At the end of its financial period all branches convert their financial statements from the currency of the host country to the currency of the home country to submit to headquarters to prepare the Company's consolidated financial statements. This follows the accounting principle of

(A) going concern   Ⓐ

(B) economic entity   Ⓑ

(C) monetary unit   Ⓒ

(D) duality.   Ⓓ

27 The cost of pens, paper and envelopes are not shown as a separate expense item in the income statement but summarised as office stationery of the White Sands Hotels. However, the remuneration to the Board of Directors is not summarised with the wages and salaries but shown separately. This adheres to the accounting principle of

(A) accruals   Ⓐ

(B) materiality   Ⓑ

(C) monetary unit   Ⓒ

(D) going concern.   Ⓓ

28 St Anns Marketing Company has had an average of 3% of its accounts receivable being uncollectable each year but no allowance is being made for the possibility of the occurrence of these uncollectable accounts for the next accounting period at the end of the current financial period. This is a breach of the

(A) accruals concept   Ⓐ

(B) going concern assumption   Ⓑ

(C) revenue recognition principle   Ⓒ

(D) prudence concept.   Ⓓ

29 Ready Car Rentals' financial year ends on 30th September. It rented a car to Nigel Frost at $1200 per month for the period January to December 2019. What is the total revenue recorded by Ready Car Rentals for the car rented to Nigel Frost at the end of its financial period in 2019?

(A) $3600   Ⓐ

(B) $4800   Ⓑ

(C) $8400   Ⓒ

(D) $10 800   Ⓓ

1.1.2 Recording Financial Information

Assets – purchase, sale, book value vs fair market value, basket purchase

1 Callender Accounting Associates sold to Chelsea Enterprises some computers that had a book value of $15 000 for $12 000. How is the loss on sale of the computers journalised?

(A) Dr: Cash $3000   Cr: Income summary $3000   Ⓐ

(B) Dr: Income summary $3000   Cr: Disposal of Office Equipment $3000   Ⓑ

(C) Dr: Disposal of Office Equipment $3000   Cr: Income summary $3000   Ⓒ

(D) Dr: Income summary $3000   Cr: Cash $3000   Ⓓ

2 Roses Decorators Limited acquired the physical assets of Gone Home Enterprises, distributing an equivalent value of ordinary shares to Gone Home Enterprises. The assets had a book value of $1 180 000 and a fair market value of $2 000 000. The transaction will be recorded by Roses Decorators Limited as

(A) Dr: Assets $1 180 000   Cr: Ordinary Shares $1 180 000   Ⓐ

(B) Dr: Assets $2 000 000   Cr: Ordinary Shares $2 000 000   Ⓑ

(C) Dr: Assets $1 180 000   Dr: Income Summary (loss) 20 000   Ⓒ
    Cr: Ordinary Shares $2 000 000

(D) Dr: Assets $2 000 000   Cr: Share Premium 20 000   Ⓓ
    Cr: Ordinary Shares $1 800 000

Items **3–4** refer to the following information

Naples Limited acquired a group of assets as a basket purchase from Bishop Holding Limited, paying $200 000. The assets and their value are listed in Table 2.1.

Table 2.1

	Fair Value $
Premises	120 000
Office Equipment	80 000
Machinery	50 000

3 The value of Machinery recorded in the books of Naples Limited is

(A) $40 000   Ⓐ

(B) $50 000   Ⓑ

(C) $64 000   Ⓒ

(D) $80 000.   Ⓓ

4 The value of Office Equipment recorded in the books of Naples Limited is

(A) $40 000   Ⓐ

(B) $50 000   Ⓑ

(C) $64 000   Ⓒ

(D) $80 000.   Ⓓ

5 A sinking fund is used to

(A) provide funds for the owners of the business ⒶA

(B) redeem a long-term debt at maturity ⒷB

(C) reinvest for the future growth of the business ⒸC

(D) assist the business should liquidity problems occur. ⒹD

6 A sinking fund is recorded in the Statement of Financial Position under the heading

(A) Current Assets ⒶA

(B) Property, Plant and Equipment ⒷB

(C) Long-term Investments ⒸC

(D) Intangible Assets. ⒹD

7 A group of doctors have paid $59 000 for start-up costs for the establishment of the Kingston Private Hospital Limited. These costs include attorney fees for preparation of memorandum and articles of association and all related documents necessary for filing for incorporation of a business, filing fees with the Registrar of Companies and training of employees in their new company. These costs are considered

(A) an expense ⒶA

(B) a current asset ⒷB

(C) a long-term investment ⒸC

(D) organisation costs. ⒹD

8 The exclusive legal right granted by government or authorised agency to a business or person that restricts others from making, using or selling its invention for a specific period is called a

(A) copyright ⒶA

(B) franchise ⒷB

(C) patent ⒸC

(D) trademark. ⒹD

9 Halfway Tree Co. purchased a patent for $1 500 000 from Stepping International for the production of its unique athletic shoes. The life of the patent is 8 years. The process for adjusting for the loss in value of the patent each year over its useful life is called

(A) depreciation

Ⓐ

(B) reconciliation

Ⓑ

(C) amortisation

Ⓒ

(D) depletion.

Ⓓ

10 Hillary Group of Companies acquired Leslie Enterprises, paying $13 000 000. The book value of net assets was $9 000 000 and their fair market value was $12 000 000. What is the value of goodwill?

(A) 0

Ⓐ

(B) $1 000 000

Ⓑ

(C) $3 000 000

Ⓒ

(D) $4 000 000

Ⓓ

Liabilities – identification and calculation

11 Gordon Enterprises received a 5-year note payable of $75 000 on 2 January 2017. It is to be repaid in equal instalments starting 2 January 2018. Which of the following is an accurate entry in the Statement of Financial Position on 31 December 2017?

(A) Note Payable $75 000 under Non-current Liabilities

Ⓐ

(B) Note Payable $60 000 under Current Liabilities

Ⓑ

(C) Note Payable $15 000 under Non-current Liabilities

Ⓒ

(D) Note Payable $15 000 under Current Liabilities

Ⓓ

Revenues – recognition, calculation and journalising

12 Make-It-Work Enterprises repaired some machines for Antigua Cooperative on 17 May 2018 and sent the invoice to the cooperative for $13 000 for the repairs on the same day. Antigua Cooperative contacted Make-It-Work Enterprises on 20 May 2018 informing the business that they had received the invoice and that payment would follow. Antigua Cooperative delivered a cheque for $7000 on 29 May 2018 to Make-It-Work Enterprises. On what date should Make-It-Work Enterprises record the revenue for repairing the machines and what value should it be?

(A) 17 May 2018 – $7000   Ⓐ

(B) 17 May 2018 – $13 000   Ⓑ

(C) 20 May 2018 – $13 000   Ⓒ

(D) 29 May 2018 – $7000   Ⓓ

13 Blue Rawls sold inventory to Boland and Sons worth $90 000. Boland and Sons paid $70 000 by cheque immediately and the balance is due. The correct journal entry for revenue by Blue Rawls is

    I Cr: Revenue $20 000

    II Cr: Revenue $70 000

    III Cr: Revenue $90 000

(A) I and II   Ⓐ

(B) II only   Ⓑ

(C) II and III   Ⓒ

(D) III only   Ⓓ

Items **14–15** refer to the following information

Mainland Pools cleans and services pools in St Kitts. The business received payment of $24 000 for its annual service contract for the calendar year 2017 with Courtley Hotel on 9 January 2017. Mainland Pools' financial year ends on 30 September 2017.

14 On 9 January 2017 how is the transaction to be journalised?

(A) Dr: Courtley Hotel $24 000   Cr: Revenue $24 000   (A)

(B) Dr: Cash $24 000   Cr: Revenue $24 000   (B)

(C) Dr: Cash $24 000   Cr: Deferred Revenue $24 000   (C)

(D) Dr: Courtley Hotel $24 000   Cr: Deferred Revenue $24 000   (D)

15 On 30 September 2017 how is revenue for Mainland Pools journalised?

(A) Dr: Courtley Hotel $6000   Cr: Revenue $6000   (A)

(B) Dr: Deferred Revenue $6000   Cr: Revenue $6000   (B)

(C) Dr: Deferred Revenue $18 000   Cr: Revenue $18 000   (C)

(D) Dr: Deferred Revenue $24 000   Cr: Revenue $24 000   (D)

Expenses – recognition, calculation and journalising

16 McLean Industries had its air-conditioning units serviced by Alpha Air-Conditioning during 2020. McLean Industries received an invoice for $19 000 dated 28 December 2020 and paid ¾ of the invoice on 31 December 2019. The journal entries to record the expense by McLean Industries for the year are

(A) Dr: Maintenance Expenses $14 250   Cr: Income Summary $14 250   (A)

(B) Dr: Income Summary $14 250   Cr: Maintenance Expenses $14 250   (B)

(C) Dr: Maintenance Expenses $19 000   Cr: Income Summary $19 000   (C)

(D) Dr: Income Summary $19 000   Cr: Maintenance Expenses $19 000   (D)

17 Barbados Building Company paid Cable Can Enterprises $24 000 during the year 2018 for providing cable and internet services. Cable Can Enterprises charges $1500 a month for providing these services. To record the deferred expense by Barbados Building Company the journal entries would be

(A) Dr: Deferred Expense $6000   Cr: Expense $6000   (A)

(B) Dr: Expense $6000   Cr: Deferred Expense $6000   (B)

(C) Dr: Expense $18 000   Cr: Deferred Expense $18 000   (C)

(D) Dr: Deferred Expense $24 000   Cr: Expense $24 000   (D)

Adjustments – depreciation, doubtful accounts, goodwill, patents and franchise

18 Laventille Sports Club has sports equipment recorded as: cost $162 000 and accumulated depreciation $42 000. Depreciation is charged at a rate of 15% per annum on the reducing (diminishing) balance basis. Which is the correct entries for the journal to record depreciation for the year?

(A) Dr: Allowance for Depreciation $24 300   Cr: Income Summary $24 300   Ⓐ

(B) Dr: Allowance for Depreciation $18 000   Cr: Income Summary $18 000   Ⓑ

(C) Dr: Income Summary $18 000   Cr: Allowance for Depreciation $18 000   Ⓒ

(D) Dr: Income Summary $24 300   Cr: Allowance for Depreciation $24 300   Ⓓ

Items **19–20** refer to the following information.

Clean Specialist Janitorial Services started business on 1 January 2019. Table 2.2 relates to the organisation.

Table 2.2

Year ending 31 December	Accounts receivable balance	Allowance for doubtful debts annual rate (%)
2019	$26 000	3%
2020	$29 000	2%

19 What are the journal entries to record the adjustment for the allowance for doubtful accounts at the end of 2019?

(A) Dr: Income Summary $200   Cr: Allowance for Doubtful Debts $200   Ⓐ

(B) Dr: Allowance for Doubtful Debts $580   Cr: Income Summary $580   Ⓑ

(C) Dr: Allowance for Doubtful Debts $780   Cr: Income Summary $780   Ⓒ

(D) Dr: Income Summary $780   Cr: Allowance for Doubtful Debts $780   Ⓓ

20 What are the journal entries to record the change in the allowance for doubtful accounts at the end of 2020?

(A) Dr: Income Summary $580   Cr: Allowance for Doubtful Debts $580   Ⓐ

(B) Dr: Allowance for Doubtful Debts $580   Cr: Income Summary $580   Ⓑ

(C) Dr: Income Summary $200   Cr: Allowance for Doubtful Debts $200   Ⓒ

(D) Dr: Allowance for Doubtful Debts $200   Cr: Income Summary $200   Ⓓ

21 The National Oil Company acquired the right to drill for oil and natural gas in an offshore block in Belize waters worth $45 000 000. The company found an estimated 20 000 000 tons of oil and gas. During the year the company extracted 5000 tons. Identify the journal entries for the depletion of the natural resource.

(A) Dr: Depletion Expense $1125   Cr: Accumulated Depletion $1125   (A)

(B) Dr: Depletion Expense $5000   Cr: Accumulated Depletion $5000   (B)

(C) Dr: Depletion Expense $10 000   Cr: Accumulated Depletion $10 000   (C)

(D) Dr: Depletion Expense $11 250   Cr: Accumulated Depletion $11 250   (D)

Capital and reserves – recognition, use, calculation and journal entries

22 The balance of profits retained at the end of the financial period is referred to as

(A) Capital Reserve   (A)

(B) Capital Expenditure   (B)

(C) Revenue Reserve   (C)

(D) Revenue Expenditure.   (D)

23 Alexander Investments Limited's financial year ended on 30 September 2021. At 31 March 2021 the company made a cash payment of interim dividend of $17 000 and at the end of the financial year the dividend payable was $23 000. The company's declared dividend was

(A) $6000   (A)

(B) $17 000   (B)

(C) $23 000   (C)

(D) $40 000.   (D)

24 Soufriere Tours Limited issued 40 000 ordinary shares at $3.00 each. The issue was fully subscribed. The par value of a share was $2.00. The journal entry to record this issue is

(A) Dr: Cash $120 000   Cr: Ordinary Shares $120 000   (A)

(B) Dr: Cash $120 000   Cr: Ordinary Shares $80 000   (B)
                            Cr: Income Summary: Operating Revenue $40 000

(C) Dr: Cash $120 000   Cr: Ordinary Shares $80 000   (C)
                            Cr: Income Summary: Other Revenue $40 000

(D) Dr: Cash $120 000   Cr: Ordinary Shares $80 000   (D)
                            Cr: Paid in Capital in Excess of Par $40 000

Items 25–26 refer to the following information

Jamaica National Bank issued 20 000 ordinary shares of par value $10 each and market value $15 each to its current ordinary shareholders only for a value of $12 each. The issue was fully subscribed.

25 What type of issue is this called?

(A) Bonus Issue   Ⓐ

(B) Rights Issue   Ⓑ

(C) General Issue   Ⓒ

(D) Treasury Stock   Ⓓ

26 The journal entries to record the issue are

(A) Dr: Cash $200 000   Cr: Ordinary Shares $200 000   Ⓐ

(B) Dr: Cash $240 000   Cr: Ordinary Shares $200 000   Ⓑ
Cr: Paid in Capital in Excess of Par $40 000

(C) Dr: Cash $300 000   Cr: Ordinary Shares $200 000   Ⓒ
Cr: Income Summary: Other Revenue $100 000

(D) Dr: Cash $300 000   Cr: Ordinary Shares $200 000   Ⓓ
Cr: Paid in Capital in Excess of Par $100 000

27 When a company buys back ordinary shares from its shareholders, they are recorded as

(A) Bonus Issue   Ⓐ

(B) Rights Issue   Ⓑ

(C) General Issue   Ⓒ

(D) Treasury Stock.   Ⓓ

Capital reserves – recognition and use

28 A building of Sammy Limited had a book value of $1 500 000. Valuators have revalued the building to $1 800 000. How is the journal for the increased value of the building recorded?

    (A) Dr: Building   Cr: Income Summary: Operating Revenue   (A)

    (B) Dr: Building   Cr: Income Summary: Other Revenue and Expenses   (B)

    (C) Dr: Building   Cr: Revaluation Reserve   (C)

    (D) Dr: Building   Cr: Non-Current Liabilities   (D)

29 Capital reserves **cannot** be used for the

    (A) issue of bonus shares to the shareholders   (A)

    (B) payment of dividends regardless of profits   (B)

    (C) writing off expenses incurred in issuing shares   (C)

    (D) financing the premium payable on redemption of shares.   (D)

1.1.3 Internal Controls

The objectives of internal controls

1 Internal controls are also called

    I administrative controls

    II accounting controls

    III cumulative controls.

    (A) I and II   (A)

    (B) I and III   (B)

    (C) II and III   (C)

    (D) I, II and III   (D)

2 Included in the major objectives of internal control are to

> **I** promote compliance with management's policies and procedures
>
> **II** safeguard the assets from wastage, theft and fraud
>
> **III** pre-number all document used in the organisation.

(A) I and II   Ⓐ

(B) I and III   Ⓑ

(C) II and III   Ⓒ

(D) I, II and III   Ⓓ

3 Which statement is not true about the purpose of internal controls?

(A) Internal controls help to promote the accomplishment of the organisation's goals and objectives.   Ⓐ

(B) Internal controls help to encourage the efficient use of the organisation's resources.   Ⓑ

(C) Internal controls help to select employees that are competent, reliable and ethical.   Ⓒ

(D) Internal controls help to ensure accurate and reliable recording and reporting of financial information.   Ⓓ

Principles of internal control systems

4 The principles of internal controls are usually divided into how many categories?

(A) 4   Ⓐ

(B) 5   Ⓑ

(C) 6   Ⓒ

(D) 7   Ⓓ

5 Which of the following is not a principle aim of internal controls?

(A) Safeguarding of the assets   Ⓐ

(B) Establishment of responsibility   Ⓑ

(C) Segregation of duties   Ⓒ

(D) Independent internal verification   Ⓓ

6 A clerk in the accounts department is responsible for the preparation and disbursement of cheques to suppliers, updating of suppliers' accounts, collection of cashed cheques and bank statements from the bank, and the preparation of the bank reconciliation statement. Which internal control principle is being violated?

(A) Establishment of responsibility Ⓐ

(B) Segregation of duties Ⓑ

(C) Documentation procedures Ⓒ

(D) Physical, mechanical and electronic controls Ⓓ

7 General Graduation Center, a clothing store, has three sales clerks, all of whom use the cash register to receive money from customers for sales made. Each sales person, however, has to enter their unique pin number to activate access to the cash register and the transaction entered can be traced to the sales person's pin number that has been entered. Each sales person logs out when they leave the cash register. Which internal control principle is being followed?

(A) Establishment of responsibility Ⓐ

(B) Segregation of duties Ⓑ

(C) Documentation procedures Ⓒ

(D) Physical, mechanical and electronic controls Ⓓ

8 Stephen, James and Associates, a law firm, provides secure employee card key access to its employees. Different levels of employees are provided with different levels of access. Employees are required to submit, in the first week of each year, the period that they will go on vacation; there are no exceptions to this rule. The vacation must be taken. The internal control principles being followed are

    I establishment of responsibility

    II physical, mechanical and electronic controls

    III other controls.

(A) I and II Ⓐ

(B) I and III Ⓑ

(C) II and III Ⓒ

(D) I, II and III Ⓓ

9 The internal control principle that states immediate supervisors and persons so trained are responsible for the checking of other staff members' work to ensure that the organisation's policies and procedures are being followed is

(A) segregation of duties Ⓐ

(B) documentation procedures Ⓑ

(C) physical, mechanical and electronic controls Ⓒ

(D) independent internal verification. Ⓓ

10 The employing of security guards, walls, gates and cameras are the internal control principle of

(A) establishment of responsibility Ⓐ

(B) other controls Ⓑ

(C) documentation procedures Ⓒ

(D) physical, mechanical and electronic controls. Ⓓ

11 Islands Commercial Bank has taken out an insurance policy against theft by tellers at its various branches. Islands Commercial Bank therefore adheres to the internal control principle of

(A) documentation procedures Ⓐ

(B) other controls Ⓑ

(C) physical mechanical and electronic controls Ⓒ

(D) independent internal verification. Ⓓ

12 Sports Alive, a sports store, has a cashier that collects cash and cheques from customers, reconciles the receipts for the day, prepares the deposit slip and deposits the monies collected into the bank's night deposit facility after work. The internal control principle being violated is

(A) establishment of responsibility Ⓐ

(B) segregation of duties Ⓑ

(C) independent internal verification Ⓒ

(D) other controls. Ⓓ

13 Tree-Are-We, manufacturers of home and office furniture, has the following policy regarding the purchase of raw materials for the manufacture of its products. Once the raw materials inventory has reached its reorder level, the stores manager sends a requisition to the procurement department for the restocking of raw materials. The procurement department prepares the purchase order in quadruplicate and distributes it as follows. The original to the supplier, one copy to the stores department, another to the accounts department, and the last copy is kept by the procurement department. When the raw materials are delivered the stores department checks the delivery against its copy of the purchase order and forwards the invoice to the accounts department for payment. Which internal control principle is being adhered to?

(A) Documentation procedures   Ⓐ

(B) Segregation of duties   Ⓑ

(C) Establishment of responsibility   Ⓒ

(D) Physical controls   Ⓓ

14 Which of the following statements are true about internal auditors?

(A) They report to the shareholders at the AGM.   Ⓐ

(B) They audit the financial statements annually.   Ⓑ

(C) They are independent of the firm they audit.   Ⓒ

(D) They are hired by management.   Ⓓ

15 External auditors are

(A) appointed and approved by the shareholders   Ⓐ

(B) appointed and approved by the Board of Directors   Ⓑ

(C) appointed and approved by management   Ⓒ

(D) appointed and approved by the accounting manager.   Ⓓ

16 External audits are carried out

(A) monthly   Ⓐ

(B) quarterly   Ⓑ

(C) half yearly   Ⓒ

(D) annually.   Ⓓ

Technology and internal controls

17 One advantage of using computers in accounting over manual accounting systems is that

(A) The information is less accurate. (A)

(B) Better accounting concepts are used. (B)

(C) There is greater storage of information. (C)

(D) GAAP is not followed. (D)

18 Entering data on forms provided by the software that generates numbers in a key field automatically, which can then be printed out, is an application of the internal control principle of documentation procedures

(A) when collecting cash (A)

(B) over accounts receivable (B)

(C) for recording inventory (C)

(D) in an EDP environment (D)

19 Sales invoices for debtors are secured in a locked drawer or cabinet. Paid invoices of debtors are stamped 'payment received', dated and filed away in a fireproof cabinet. This process is an application of the internal control principle of physical, mechanical and electronic controls

(A) when collecting cash (A)

(B) over accounts receivable (B)

(C) for recording inventory (C)

(D) in an EDP environment. (D)

20 Internal controls may fail where

(A) There is collusion among employees. (A)

(B) There is segregation of duties. (B)

(C) The internal auditor checks the systems periodically. (C)

(D) The company is highly mechanised. (D)

Various forms of business organisations

1 Which of the following is NOT a characteristic of a partnership?

(A) Mutual agency   (A)

(B) Continuous life   (B)

(C) Limited life   (C)

(D) Co-ownership of property   (D)

2 Which of the following institutions is regarded as a non-governmental organisation (NGO)?

(A) A church   (A)

(B) A credit union   (B)

(C) A family business   (C)

(D) A public corporation   (D)

3 An organisation formed by a group of persons to represent themselves is known as a

(A) corporation   (A)

(B) cooperative   (B)

(C) partnership   (C)

(D) sole proprietorship.   (D)

4 Which of the following type of owners bears all the risk or possible losses of that business?

(A) A sole trader   (A)

(B) One or two partners   (B)

(C) Shareholders   (C)

(D) Members   (D)

Advantages and disadvantages of forms of organisations

5 Social clubs and charitable organisations are examples of

(**A**) cooperatives   Ⓐ

(**B**) partnership   Ⓑ

(**C**) sole proprietorship organisation   Ⓒ

(**D**) non-governmental organisations (NGOs) or non-profit organisations.   Ⓓ

6 The advantages of a Corporation are

    I they have continuous life

    II they can raise more money

    III some shareholders have limited liability.

(**A**) I only   Ⓐ

(**B**) I and II   Ⓑ

(**C**) II and III   Ⓒ

(**D**) I, II and III   Ⓓ

7 Which of the following features distinguishes a Partnership from a Limited Liability Company (Corporation)?

    I Operations are conducted by partners

    II Operations are conducted by a Board of Directors

    III Pays corporation tax on net income

(**A**) I only   Ⓐ

(**B**) II   Ⓑ

(**C**) I and III   Ⓒ

(**D**) II and III   Ⓓ

Distinguish between private, public and statutory corporations

8 Which of the following would NOT be considered as a feature of a public corporation?

(A) Few shareholders (A)

(B) Thousands of shareholders (B)

(C) Shares are traded on the stock market (C)

(D) Capital composed of shareholders' equity and financial institutions (D)

9 Statutory corporations

    I have a Board of Directors appointed by a government minister

    II are owned by the government

    III are established by an Act of Parliament.

(A) I only (A)

(B) I and II (B)

(C) II and III (C)

(D) I, II and III (D)

10 An enterprise where shares are NOT available for purchase in the stock market is known as a

(A) private company (A)

(B) public company (B)

(C) statutory corporation (C)

(D) government-run organisation. (D)

1.2.2 Preparation and Presentation of Statement of Comprehensive Income

1 Which of the following standards identifies the four (4) main categories of revenue?

(A) International Accounting Standards (IAS) 1 (Section 3 of the IFRS for SMEs) (A)

(B) International Accounting Standards (IAS) 1 (Section 6 of the IFRS for SMEs) (B)

(C) International Accounting Standards (IAS) 2 (Section 13 of the IFRS for SMEs) (C)

(D) International Accounting Standards (IAS) 18 (Section 23 of the IFRS for SMEs) (D)

2 The inventory valuation method NOT considered as an acceptable format for International Accounting Standards (IAS) 2 (Sections 13 of the IFRS for SMEs) is

(A) first in first out (FIFO) (A)

(B) last in first out (LIFO) (B)

(C) specific identification (C)

(D) weighted average. (D)

Items **3–4** refer to the information shown below.

Herrera Limited provided you with the information shown in Table 2.1.

Table 2.1

Date	Details	Unit quantity	Unit cost
June	Beginning inventory	300	$15.00
July	Purchases	200	$10.00
August	Purchases	300	$14.00
September	Purchases	100	$15.00

Goods issued for the year = 600.

3 Using the first in first out (FIFO) method of inventory valuation, the total value of the closing inventory is

(A) $4065 (A)

(B) $4300 (B)

(C) $4500 (C)

(D) $8130. (D)

28

4 Using the weighted average method of inventory valuation, the total value of the closing inventory is

(A) $4065   (A)

(B) $4300   (B)

(C) $4500   (C)

(D) $8130.   (D)

5 It is the end of Peter's financial year. On 1 January 2015, his beginning inventory was $8000. He wants to transfer (close) the inventory to the Income Statement. Which of the following journal entries is correct?

(A) Dr: Income Summary $8000   Cr: Inventory $8000   (A)

(B) Dr: Income Summary $8000   Cr: Cash $8000   (B)

(C) Dr: Inventory $8000   Cr: Income Summary $8000   (C)

(D) Dr: Cash $8000   Cr: Income Summary $8000   (D)

6 Kerron started the year 2014 with an office supplies inventory of $9000. At the end of the year the office supplies inventory was $4000. The journal entry to record the value of office supplies consumed is

(A) Dr: Office supplies expense $4000   Cr: Office supplies inventory $4000   (A)

(B) Dr: Office supplies inventory $4000   Cr: Office supplies expense $4000   (B)

(C) Dr: Office supplies expense $5000   Cr: Office supplies inventory $5000   (C)

(D) Dr: Office supplies inventory $5000   Cr: Office supplies expense $5000   (D)

7 Which of the following formulae determines profit for the year in a multiple step Statement of Comprehensive Income?

(A) Profit before tax + Income tax expense   (A)

(B) Profit before tax − Income tax expense   (B)

(C) Profit before tax + Cost of goods sold   (C)

(D) Profit before tax + Dividends   (D)

8 Which of the following statements determines a firm's net income or net loss?

(A) Statement of Cashflow   (A)

(B) Statement of Owner's Equity   (B)

(C) Statement of Financial Position   (C)

(D) Statement of Comprehensive Income   (D)

Item **9** refers to the following information:

John began operations with	$30 000
Additional capital invested	$30 000
Withdrawals for personal use	$10 000
Closing capital	$60 000

9 John's profit earnings for the period is

(A) $10 000   (A)

(B) $30 000   (B)

(C) $60 000   (C)

(D) $70 000.   (D)

10 Which of the following standards identifies the elements shown in a statement of retained earnings?

(A) International Accounting Standards (IAS) 1 (Section 3 of IFRS for SMEs)   (A)

(B) International Accounting Standards (IAS) 1 (Section 6 of IFRS for SMEs)   (B)

(C) International Accounting Standards (IAS) 2 (Section 13 of IFRS for SMEs)   (C)

(D) International Accounting Standards (IAS) 18 (Section 23 of IFRS for SMEs)   (D)

11 Revenue reserves are profits set aside for

     I future growth

     II future existence (continuance)

    III distribution as dividends.

(**A**) I only   Ⓐ

(**B**) II only   Ⓑ

(**C**) I and III   Ⓒ

(**D**) I, II and III   Ⓓ

12 When determining the lower of cost and net realisable value (NRV), a company should include

     I estimated selling price

     II further costs to completion

    III selling and distribution costs of inventory.

(**A**) I only   Ⓐ

(**B**) I and II   Ⓑ

(**C**) I and III   Ⓒ

(**D**) I, II and III   Ⓓ

13 The purchase cost of inventory includes

     I the purchase price

     II Free on Board (FOB) destination

    III import duties and taxes.

(**A**) I only   Ⓐ

(**B**) II only   Ⓑ

(**C**) I and II   Ⓒ

(**D**) I and III   Ⓓ

Items **14–15** refer to the cost of goods sold (cost of sales) multiple step format statement shown in Table 2.2.

Table 2.2

	$	$
Opening inventory		9000
Purchases	4000	
Less Purchases returns and allowances	(1000)	
Less purchases discounts	(800)	
Net purchases	2200	
Add Carriage inwards	I	
Cost of goods purchased		2600
Cost of goods available for sale		11 600
II		(3000)
Cost of goods sold		8600

14 What sum of money is represented by I?

(A) $400

(B) $2200

(C) $6400

(D) $9000

Ⓐ

Ⓑ

Ⓒ

Ⓓ

15 What does II represent in the cost of goods sold multistep format statement?

(A) Sales

(B) Dividends

(C) Withdrawals

(D) Ending inventory

Ⓐ

Ⓑ

Ⓒ

Ⓓ

Statement of Changes in Equity using established accounting guidelines

<u>Item **1**</u> refers to the following information.

Bengie started business in 2012. He supplied the listing for 2014 below.

Profit for the year	$80 000
Retained earnings balance brought down	$90 000
Prior year adjustment understatement of 2013 depreciation	$20 000
Dividends declared	$20 000

1 The balance of retained earnings for 2014 is

(A) $110 000   Ⓐ

(B) $130 000   Ⓑ

(C) $150 000   Ⓒ

(D) $170 000.   Ⓓ

2 The preparation of Statement of Changes of Owner's Equity is governed by

(A) International Accounting Standards (IAS) 1 (Section 3 of IFRS for SMEs)   Ⓐ

(B) International Accounting Standards (IAS) 1 (Section 4 of IFRS for SMEs)   Ⓑ

(C) International Accounting Standards (IAS) 1 (Section 6 of IFRS for SMEs)   Ⓒ

(D) International Accounting Standards (IAS) 1 (Section 13 of IFRS for SMEs).   Ⓓ

Statement of Financial Position using established accounting guidelines

3 Which of the following standards emphasises that a liability is a present obligation of an entity arising from past events?

(A) International Accounting Standards (IAS) 1 (Section 3 from IFRS for SMEs)   Ⓐ

(B) International Accounting Standards (IAS) 1 (Section 4 from IFRS for SMEs)   Ⓑ

(C) International Accounting Standards (IAS) 1 (Section 8 from IFRS for SMEs)   Ⓒ

(D) International Accounting Standards (IAS) 1 (Section 22 from IFRS for SMEs).   Ⓓ

4 The standard which applies to recognition and recording of the cost and depreciation of property, plant and equipment in the financial statements is

(A) International Accounting Standards (IAS) 1 (Section 22 from IFRS for SMEs) Ⓐ

(B) International Accounting Standards (IAS) 2 (Section 13 from IFRS for SMEs) Ⓑ

(C) International Accounting Standards (IAS) 16 (Section 17 for IFRS for SMEs) Ⓒ

(D) International Accounting Standards (IAS) 18 (Section 23 for IFRS for SMEs). Ⓓ

Items **5–7** refer to the following information

Cost of equipment (year end 2014)	$100 000
Allowance for depreciation (January 1, 2014)	$25 000
Rate of depreciation	10%
Depreciation method	Reducing balance

5 What is the annual depreciation for 2014?

(A) $2500 Ⓐ

(B) $7500 Ⓑ

(C) $9000 Ⓒ

(D) $10 000 Ⓓ

6 The accumulated depreciation of equipment for 2014 is

(A) $27 500 Ⓐ

(B) $32 500 Ⓑ

(C) $34 000 Ⓒ

(D) $35 000. Ⓓ

7 The net book value of the equipment for 2014 is

(A) $65 000   Ⓐ

(B) $66 000   Ⓑ

(C) $67 500   Ⓒ

(D) $72 500.   Ⓓ

8 The items used to prepare the Statement of Financial Position for records that are incomplete include

    I payables paid

    II receivables collected

    III current and acid test ratios.

(A) I only   Ⓐ

(B) II only   Ⓑ

(C) I and II   Ⓒ

(D) I, II and III   Ⓓ

9 The Statement of Changes in Owner's Equity provides

(A) the ending figure/balances for the Statement of Financial Position   Ⓐ

(B) report on assets, liabilities and owner' equity   Ⓑ

(C) information on profit or loss made   Ⓒ

(D) report on a firm's financing activities.   Ⓓ

Financial statements from incomplete records or where records are deficient or erroneous

10 Accounts receivable control accounts may be used to calculate

(A) closing capital   Ⓐ

(B) credit purchases   Ⓑ

(C) credit sales   Ⓒ

(D) amounts paid for payables.   Ⓓ

11 Mark-up is equal to

(A) gross profit ÷ sales   Ⓐ

(B) gross profit ÷ cost of sales   Ⓑ

(C) sales – gross profit   Ⓒ

(D) cost of goods available for sale – closing inventory.   Ⓓ

12 Accounts payable control accounts may be used to calculate

     I credit purchases

     II amounts collected from receivable

     III amounts paid from payables.

(A) I only   Ⓐ

(B) II only   Ⓑ

(C) I and II   Ⓒ

(D) I and III   Ⓓ

Item 13 refers to the following balances from Dominique's books for Accounts Receivable.

Opening balance	$100 000
Receipts collected for receivable	$300 000
Closing balance	$50 000

13 The total credit sales amount is

(A) $100 000   Ⓐ

(B) $150 000   Ⓑ

(C) $250 000   Ⓒ

(D) $350 000.   Ⓓ

Items **14–15** refer to the following information.

Salaries paid during the year $320 000

The monthly salaries bill $20 000

14 The salaries expense for the year is

     (A) $20 000   Ⓐ

     (B) $240 000   Ⓑ

     (C) $320 000   Ⓒ

     (D) $360 000.   Ⓓ

15 The total prepaid salaries for the period is

     (A) $20 000   Ⓐ

     (B) $40 000   Ⓑ

     (C) $60 000   Ⓒ

     (D) $80 000.   Ⓓ

16 The credit purchase of an electronic scanner from Briget computers for $10 000 has been completely omitted from the records. Which of the following journal entry is correct?

     (A) Dr: Electronic Scanner $10 000   Cr: Creditor – Briget $10 000   Ⓐ

     (B) Dr: Debtor – Briget $10 000   Cr: Electronic Scanner $10 000   Ⓑ

     (C) Dr: Electronic Scanner $10 000   Cr: Cash $10 000   Ⓒ

     (D) Dr: Creditor –Briget $10 000   Cr: Electronic Scanner $10 000   Ⓓ

17 The temporary account created when a Trial Balance's totals do NOT agree is known as a

     (A) Personal account   Ⓐ

     (B) Suspense account   Ⓑ

     (C) Reconciliation account   Ⓒ

     (D) Control account.   Ⓓ

18 The financial statement used to show the calculation of Capital and Net Profit for incomplete records is known as

(A) Statement of Financial Position

(B) Statement of Affairs

(C) Statement of Comprehensive Income

(D) Statement of Changes of Owner's Equity.

Ⓐ Ⓑ Ⓒ Ⓓ

19 A cheque paid to Yvette for $2000 had been correctly entered in the cash account but had been omitted from Yvette's account. The journal entry to correct the error is

(A) Dr: Yvette $2000   Cr: Bank $2000

(B) Dr: Bank $2000   Cr: Yvette $2000

(C) Dr: Yvette $2000   Cr: Suspense $2000

(D) Dr: Suspense $2000   Cr: Yvette $2000

Ⓐ Ⓑ Ⓒ Ⓓ

20 Which of the following journals (day books) provide dishonoured cheques and bad debts for the preparation of control accounts?

    I General Journal

    II Sales Journal

    III Sales Returns Journal

(A) I only

(B) II only

(C) II and III

(D) I, II and III

Ⓐ Ⓑ Ⓒ Ⓓ

21 Set off (contra or transfer) entries in control accounts imply

      I customer may also be a supplier

      II errors made in customer's account

      III an overpaid sum of money.

(A) I only   Ⓐ

(B) II only   Ⓑ

(C) I and III   Ⓒ

(D) I, II and III   Ⓓ

<u>Items **22–23**</u> refer to the following information.

In January Kaleb invested $200 000 from his private savings account into his business bank account. At the end of the first year, Kaleb received a $400 000 loan from his banker to expand the business. He presented the following information at the end of the year.

Motor van	$300 000
Stock	$70 000
Bank	$15 000
Office furniture	$40 000
Telephone bill unpaid	$3000

22 Kaleb's closing capital is

(A) $22 000   Ⓐ

(B) $25 000   Ⓑ

(C) $40 000   Ⓒ

(D) $200 000.   Ⓓ

23 Kaleb's net profit or loss is

(A) Profit $22 000   Ⓐ

(B) Loss $22 000   Ⓑ

(C) Profit $178 000   Ⓒ

(D) Loss $178 000.   Ⓓ

1 The financial statements prepared by Cooperatives are

    I Receipts and Payments

    II Income and Expenditure

    III Statement of Financial Position

(A) I only   Ⓐ

(B) II only   Ⓑ

(C) I and II   Ⓒ

(D) I, II and III   Ⓓ

Items **2–3** refer to the following information.

Wellness Cooperative Society Limited presented the balances shown in Table 4.1.

Table 4.1

	$
Loan interest	8000
Share capital	300 000
Sales	2 000 000
Honoraria paid	30 000
Fixtures	100 000
Cash at bank	900 000
Undistributed surplus	80 000
Insurance expense paid	5000
General expenses paid	10 000
Purchases	800 000
Salaries and wages	30 000
Provision for depreciation	20 000
10% – 15-year mortgage	200 000

2 The firm's total loan interest for the period is

(A) $8000   Ⓐ

(B) $12 000   Ⓑ

(C) $20 000   Ⓒ

(D) $28 000.   Ⓓ

3 The firm's net profit for the year is

(A) $80 000   Ⓐ

(B) $95 000   Ⓑ

(C) $1 105 000   Ⓒ

(D) $1 200 000.   Ⓓ

<u>Items **4–5**</u> refer to the information given below.

Lesley's Chorale has 300 members, each of whom pay $150 monthly as subscriptions. 20 members owe one-month balance as subscriptions. Total cash received for monthly subscriptions was $40 000.

4 The amount to be transferred to the Income and Expenditure account is

(A) $3000   Ⓐ

(B) $40 000   Ⓑ

(C) $45 000   Ⓒ

(D) $48 000.   Ⓓ

5 In which section of the balance sheet would the closing balance of the subscriptions accounts be shown?

(A) Current assets   Ⓐ

(B) Current liabilities   Ⓑ

(C) Long-term assets   Ⓒ

(D) Long-term liabilities   Ⓓ

6 A bank reconciliation statement ensures that the correct bank balance is shown in the

(A) Statement of Owners' Equity   Ⓐ

(B) Statement of Comprehensive Income   Ⓑ

(C) Statement of Cashflow   Ⓒ

(D) Statement of Financial Position.   Ⓓ

7 The financial statement which shows revenue receipts and revenue expenditures for non-profit organisations is known as

(A) Statement of Comprehensive Income   Ⓐ

(B) Statement of Changes of Owners Equity   Ⓑ

(C) Receipts and Payments   Ⓒ

(D) Statement of Financial Position.   Ⓓ

8 The accounting term replacing 'Capital' in non-profit organisations is known as

(A) Current accounts   Ⓐ

(B) Shareholders' Equity   Ⓑ

(C) Reserves   Ⓒ

(D) Accumulated Fund.   Ⓓ

9 The records of non-profit organisations are made up of

     I Receipts and Payments

     II Income and Expenditure

     III Statement of Financial Position.

(A) I only   Ⓐ

(B) II only   Ⓑ

(C) I and II   Ⓒ

(D) I, II and III   Ⓓ

10 A Receipts and Payments account shows a summary of

(A) Cash and Bank accounts   (A)

(B) Subscriptions account   (B)

(C) Accumulated depreciations account   (C)

(D) Allowance for doubtful account.   (D)

11 Which of the following accounts would be used to record special fund-raising activities in a non-profit organisation?

(A) Trading account   (A)

(B) Subscription account   (B)

(C) Receipts and Payments account   (C)

(D) Income and Expenditure account   (D)

12 Subscriptions paid in advance are shown in the

  I Subscription account

  II Balance Sheet

  III Current account.

(A) I only   (A)

(B) II only   (B)

(C) I and II   (C)

(D) I and III   (D)

Items **13–14** refer to the information listed below.

Stockholder's equity (extract) is reported as in Table 4.2.

Table 4.2

Paid in Capital	$
Common stock, $0.10 par, 10 000 shares authorised; 2000 shares outstanding	200
Paid in capital in excess of par – common	<u>49 800</u>
	50 000
Retained earnings	<u>28 000</u>
	78 000
Less Treasury stock at cost (100 shares @ $20)	<u>(2000)</u>
Total Stockholder's equity	<u>76 000</u>

13 The journal entry to account for Treasury stock is

    (A) Dr: Treasury stock $200   Cr: Cash $200   Ⓐ

    (B) Dr: Cash $200   Cr: Treasury stock $200   Ⓑ

    (C) Dr: Cash $2000   Cr: Treasury stock $2000   Ⓒ

    (D) Dr: Treasury stock $2000   Cr: Cash $2000   Ⓓ

14 What does I represent in the Stockholder's Equity Extract?

    (A) Sub total   Ⓐ

    (B) Total liabilities   Ⓑ

    (C) Total Shareholder's equity and reserves   Ⓒ

    (D) Total paid in capital   Ⓓ

Items **15–17** refer to the information given below.

The Stockholder's Equity and Reserves of McSween Company balance is as follows:

Common Stock ($1.00 par value)	$10 000
Additional Capital paid in	$19 000
Retained Earnings	$71 000
Total	$100 000

15 The Company issued two bonus shares for every one held. The total value of the bonus shares issued is

(A) $10 000

(B) $20 000

(C) $30 000

(D) $100 000.

Ⓐ Ⓑ Ⓒ Ⓓ

16 Subsequent to the bonus issue above, the Company issued 1 rights issue share for every 5 held. The total value of the rights shares issued is

(A) $6000

(B) $10 000

(C) $20 000

(D) $30 000

Ⓐ Ⓑ Ⓒ Ⓓ

17 The new balances for the Stockholder's Equity and Reserves are

(A) Ordinary Shares $36 000; Additional Capital $0;
Retained Earnings $70 000

(B) Ordinary Shares $36 000; Additional Capital $19 000;
Retained Earnings $71 000

(C) Ordinary Shares $10 000; Additional Capital $19 000;
Retained Earnings $71 000

(D) Ordinary Shares $10 000; Additional Capital $0;
Retained Earnings $70 000.

Ⓐ Ⓑ Ⓒ Ⓓ

Items **18–20** refer to the information listed in Table 4.3.

Table 4.3

Sales revenues	$150 000
Selling expenses	$10 000
Other expenses	$15 000
Finance costs	$8000
Cost of goods sold	$80 000
Administrative expenses	$20 000
Other revenues	$20 000
Corporation tax rate	20%

18 The profit before tax (PBT) is

(A) $29 600   (A)

(B) $37 000   (B)

(C) $53 000   (C)

(D) $90 000.   (D)

19 Corporation tax for the year is

(A) $7400   (A)

(B) $29 600   (B)

(C) $37 000   (C)

(D) $53 000.   (D)

20 The profit for the year is

(A) $29 600   (A)

(B) $37 000   (B)

(C) $53 000   (C)

(D) $90 000.   (D)

Changes in partnership for admission, retirement and dissolution

1 Which of the following BEST describes the partnership term 'Interest on Capital'?

(A) Rewards given to each partner for the amount of capital contributed.   Ⓐ

(B) The agreed profit and loss shared among partners.   Ⓑ

(C) Charge placed on individual partners for assets withdrawn from the partnership company.   Ⓒ

(D) The amount to be paid as a compensation to each partner.   Ⓓ

The following refers to <u>item 2</u>.

Jack and John started their partnership in 2014. They agreed to contribute an equal amount of capital and to share profits and losses equally. The total capital will be $900 000 and they will invest any differences in cash. The partners agree to contribute the assets as shown in Table 5.1.

Table 5.1

	Book value $	Fair market value $
Jack		
Machinery	300 000	400 000
Furniture	200 000	100 000
John		
Inventory	200 000	150 000
Equipment	50 000	40 000

2 The total cash contribution required is

(A) $210 000   Ⓐ

(B) $690 000   Ⓑ

(C) $900 000   Ⓒ

(D) $1 800 000.   Ⓓ

3 Joey, one of the partners of ParaLegal, has capital of $100 000. Joey decides to sell her share in the partnership to Jilly for $120 000 cash. The other partners at ParaLegal have agreed to admit Jilly in the partnership. Which of the following is the correct journal entry to record Jilly's purchase of interest in the company?

(A) Dr: Other Partners $100 000   Cr: Capital Joey $100 000   Ⓐ

(B) Dr: Other Partners $100 000   Cr: Cash $100 000   Ⓑ

(C) Dr: Joey Capital $120 000   Cr: Jilly Capital $120 000   Ⓒ

(D) Dr: Joey Capital $100 000   Cr: Jilly Capital $100 000   Ⓓ

4 The procedural steps for recording goodwill created are

     I Make journal entry to admit new partner.

     II Calculate partnership goodwill.

     III Make journal entry for goodwill created.

(A) I, II and III   Ⓐ

(B) II, I and III   Ⓑ

(C) III, II and I   Ⓒ

(D) I, III and II   Ⓓ

The following information refers to items **5–6**.

Gabby and Naomi are in partnership with $150 000 capital each, sharing profits and losses equally. On 31 December, they agree to admit Cian for 1/5 interest in the partnership upon investment of $100 000.

5 The amount of goodwill is

(A) $100 000   Ⓐ

(B) $300 000   Ⓑ

(C) $400 000   Ⓒ

(D) $500 000.   Ⓓ

6 The journal entry to record Cian's investment is

(A) Dr: Cash $250 000   Cr: Cian's Capital $250 000   Ⓐ

(B) Dr: Cian's Capital $100 000   Cr: Cash $100 000   Ⓑ

(C) Dr: Cian's Capital $250 000   Cr: Cash $250 000   Ⓒ

(D) Dr: Cash $100 000   Cr: Cian's Capital $100 000   Ⓓ

7 Denis, Franklyn and Ian are in partnership. Ian decides to retire from the company. The steps to close the business accounts for the retirement are

    I Check to see if the assets have changed in value.

    II Make journal entries to revalue assets.

    III Share the balance of the revaluation among existing partners.

(A) I, III and II   Ⓐ

(B) I, II and III   Ⓑ

(C) III, II and I   Ⓒ

(D) II, III and I   Ⓓ

The following information refers to <u>items **8–10**</u>.

Board and Liner are partners of a partnership business, sharing profits and losses in the ratio 1:2 respectively. In January their capitals were Board $80 000 and Liner $75 000. During the year, they agree to admit Wood upon an investment of $300 000 for 1/5 interest in the business.

8 What is the total amount invested in the partnership to date?

(A) $75 000   Ⓐ

(B) $80 000   Ⓑ

(C) $150 000   Ⓒ

(D) $455 000.   Ⓓ

9 Wood's 1/5 interest in the business is

(A) $25 000   Ⓐ

(B) $26 667   Ⓑ

(C) $91 000   Ⓒ

(D) $100 000.   Ⓓ

10 The total bonus to be divided between Board and Liner is

(A) $91 000   Ⓐ

(B) $100 000   Ⓑ

(C) $209 000   Ⓒ

(D) $300 000.   Ⓓ

11 Which of the following journal entries is used to close a retiring partnership capital account?

(A) Dr: Capital account   Cr: Cash account   Ⓐ

(B) Dr: Cash account   Cr: Capital account   Ⓑ

(C) Dr: Current account   Cr: Cash account   Ⓒ

(D) Dr: Cash account   Cr: Current account   Ⓓ

12 A business partnership may dissolve for a variety of reasons, such as

     I admission

     II bankruptcy

     III sale or conversion.

(A) I only   Ⓐ

(B) II only   Ⓑ

(C) I and II   Ⓒ

(D) I, II and III   Ⓓ

13 Lynette and Jewel are in partnership, sharing profits and losses in the ratio 3:2 respectively. Lynette receives a salary of $6000 per annum. The net profit for the year is $26 000. Lynette and Jewel's shares of profit are

(A) Lynette $10 000   Jewel $10 000   Ⓐ

(B) Lynette $12 000   Jewel $8 000   Ⓑ

(C) Lynette $18 000   Jewel $8 000   Ⓒ

(D) Lynette $26 000   Jewel $26 000   Ⓓ

14 A partnership may be terminated if

(A) a partnership agreement is not in writing   Ⓐ

(B) a partner dies   Ⓑ

(C) a partner exercises mutual agency   Ⓒ

(D) a partner goes on vacation.   Ⓓ

15 Lennox and Algene formed a partnership, contributing $100 000 and $50 000 respectively. They agree to 10% interest of each partner's capital balance at the beginning of the year, with sharing of income equally. The income for the first year is $50 000. The amount of income each partner will receive is

(A) $10 000   Ⓐ

(B) $17 500   Ⓑ

(C) $22 000   Ⓒ

(D) $27 000.   Ⓓ

16 Dyann and Gaynelle operate a partnership business, sharing the earnings equally. Dyann has $48 000 invested in the business and Gaynelle has $42 000 as her investment. They agreed to allow Gay a one-fifth investment and a one-fifth share of the investment of $50 000. Gay's equity is

(A) $25 000   Ⓐ

(B) $28 000   Ⓑ

(C) $45 000   Ⓒ

(D) $70 000.   Ⓓ

17 Which of the following is an example of a non-judicial dissolution issue in a partnership?

(A) Completion of purpose (A)

(B) Breach of the partnership agreement (B)

(C) When one partner becomes permanently incapable of handling matters (C)

(D) When one partner gets involved in illegal issues (D)

18 Which of the following accounts is used as a temporary account for incorporation of a partnership business?

(A) Valuation adjustment (Realisation) account (A)

(B) Share capital account (B)

(C) Partners' capital account (C)

(D) Partners current account (D)

19 The steps for incorporation of a partnership business are

    I adjust to fair market value

    II accumulate gains/losses

    III share the balance and transfer to capital accounts.

(A) I, III, and II (A)

(B) II, III and I (B)

(C) I, II and III (C)

(D) III, I and II (D)

20 The steps of liquidation are

     I pay partners

     II sell assets

     III pay liabilities.

(A) II, III and I   (A)

(B) I, III and II   (B)

(C) II, I and III   (C)

(D) III, II and I   (D)

21 The steps for recording the creation of a partnership are as follows

     I Add assets and liabilities of each partner.

     II Identify fair market value of assets of each partner.

     III Calculate and create capital accounts for each partner.

(A) I, III and II   (A)

(B) II, I and III   (B)

(C) III, II and I   (C)

(D) I, II and III   (D)

22 Tiffany, Priya and Akousa formed a partnership. They agreed to share profits and losses equally. At the end of the second year, the business incurred a remaining loss of $39 000. The journal entry to record the loss shared among the partners is

(A) Dr: Cash $39 000   (A)
Cr: Tiffany $13 000, Priya $13 000, Akousa $13 000

(B) Dr: Tiffany $13 000, Priya $13 000, Akousa $13 000   (B)
Cr: Cash $39 000

(C) Dr: Income Summary $39 000   (C)
Cr: Tiffany $13 000, Priya $13 000, Akousa $13 000

(D) Dr: Tiffany $13 000, Priya $13 000, Akousa $13 000   (D)
Cr: Income Summary $39 000.

1 Which IAS requires an entity to prepare a statement of cashflows?

(A) IAS 1   Ⓐ

(B) IAS 2   Ⓑ

(C) IAS 7   Ⓒ

(D) IAS 10   Ⓓ

2 Which items are considered cash and cash equivalents in the preparation of a statement of cashflows?

     I Bank overdraft

     II Marketable securities

     III Cash at bank

(A) I and II   Ⓐ

(B) I and III   Ⓑ

(C) II and III   Ⓒ

(D) I, II and III   Ⓓ

3 Which item is NOT considered a cash or cash equivalent item?

(A) Short-term investment   Ⓐ

(B) Bank overdraft   Ⓑ

(C) Accounts receivable   Ⓒ

(D) Cash in hand   Ⓓ

4 Which is a complete list of the subheads of the statement of cashflows?

(A) Current activities, operating activities and financing activities   Ⓐ

(B) Operating activities, investing activities and financing activities   Ⓑ

(C) Financing activities, current activities and fixed activities   Ⓒ

(D) Investing activities, fixed activities and financing activities   Ⓓ

5 The statement of cashflows is also known as

(A) Statement of Comprehensive Income   Ⓐ

(B) Statement of Changes in Equity   Ⓑ

(C) Statement of Financial Position   Ⓒ

(D) Statement of Changes in Financial Position.   Ⓓ

6 Changes in the organisation's cashflow based on the normal operations of the business and changes in working capital is recorded under which subheading of the cashflow statement?

(A) Operating activities   Ⓐ

(B) Financing inflows   Ⓑ

(C) Financing activities   Ⓒ

(D) Investing activities   Ⓓ

7 In the statement of cashflows, a gain on sale of a non-current asset is considered

(A) an inflow under investing activities   Ⓐ

(B) an outflow under operating activities   Ⓑ

(C) a non-cashflow under operating activities   Ⓒ

(D) a non-cashflow under investing activities.   Ⓓ

8 In the statement of cashflows, the loss on sale of a non-current asset should be

(A) added to profit before tax and interest   Ⓐ

(B) included as a change in working capital   Ⓑ

(C) added under investing activities   Ⓒ

(D) deducted under investing activities.   Ⓓ

9 The proceeds of a sale of machinery from a factory is considered

(A) a change in working capital   Ⓐ

(B) a cash inflow under financing activities   Ⓑ

(C) a cash inflow under investing activities   Ⓒ

(D) a decrease in operating activities.   Ⓓ

The data shown in Table 1.1 refers to <u>items **10–13**</u>.

Table 1.1

Purchase of a motor van $15 000	Acquisition of land through the issue of 20 000 ordinary shares to the land owners at par $2.00 for $50 000
Net Income $29 000	Net Increase in current liabilities $4500
Tax for the year $4000	Decrease in note payable $6000
Dividend Income $6000	Proceeds from issuance of ordinary shares $16 000
Interest expense for the year $1500	Interest income received $1200
Depreciation for the year $1750	Net Increase in current assets except cash $6000
Tax paid $3200	Interest paid $1200
Proceeds from sale of equipment $6000	Gain on sale of equipment $900

10 What is the value of the profit before interest and tax?

(A) $26 200   Ⓐ

(B) $26 500   Ⓑ

(C) $27 000   Ⓒ

(D) $27 300   Ⓓ

11 What is the value of the net cashflow from operating activities?

(A) $22 250   Ⓐ

(B) $23 950   Ⓑ

(C) $24 750   Ⓒ

(D) $25 050   Ⓓ

12 Where is the item "Acquisition of land through the issue of 20 000 ordinary shares to the land owners at par $2.00 for $50 000" identified in the financial statements?

(A) An adjusting non-cash operating activity (A)

(B) An investing activity (B)

(C) A financing activity (C)

(D) In the notes under 'A significant non-cash investing and financing activity' (D)

13 What is the value of the net cashflow from investing activities?

(A) $900 (A)

(B) ($900) (B)

(C) $1800 (C)

(D) ($1800) (D)

14 The statement of cashflows can help the user of the general purpose financial statement

    I predict future cashflows

    II evaluate management's cash decisions

    III determine future profits.

(A) I and II (A)

(B) I and III (B)

(C) II and III (C)

(D) I, II and III (D)

15 Significant non-cash investing and/or financing activities include which of the following items?

    I Acquisition of a non-current asset by assuming a note payable

    II Conversion of debt to equity

    III Acquiring a business through the issue of equity

(A) I and II (A)

(B) I and III (B)

(C) II and III (C)

(D) I, II and III (D)

Theory

1 Which group of ratios can be used to analyse a business' ability to meet its short-term obligations?

(A) Activity ratios   Ⓐ

(B) Liquidity ratios   Ⓑ

(C) Profitability ratios   Ⓒ

(D) Solvency ratios   Ⓓ

2 Which group of ratios will a bank use in determining to provide a firm with long-term financing?

(A) Activity ratios   Ⓐ

(B) Liquidity ratios   Ⓑ

(C) Profitability ratios   Ⓒ

(D) Solvency ratios   Ⓓ

Activity ratios

The following information refers to <u>items 3–5</u>.

The partnership, Paul, Small and Celestine, provide balances and data from their financial statements for 2019 as shown in Table 2.1.

Table 2.1

Sales $140 000	Cost of sales = 80% of sales
Opening Inventory $35 000	Closing Inventory = an increase of 10% over opening inventory

3 What is the value of closing inventory?

(A) $30 800   Ⓐ

(B) $31 500   Ⓑ

(C) $36 750   Ⓒ

(D) $38 500   Ⓓ

4 The value of average stock is

(A) $31 500   (A)

(B) $36 750   (B)

(C) $38 500   (C)

(D) $56 000.   (D)

5 The partnership's stock turnover is

(A) 2.91 times   (A)

(B) 3.05 times   (B)

(C) 3.81 times   (C)

(D) 3.63 times.   (D)

The information below relates to <u>items **6–7**</u>.

The partnership Robert, Raphael and Rajkumar provided an extract of balances of their financial statements as in Table 2.2. All of the business' sales are on credit.

Table 2.2

	$
Sales	120 000
Accounts Receivable 1 January 2016	25 000
Accounts Receivable 31 December 2016	15 000
Cost of Sales	80 000
Accounts Payable 1 January 2016	20 000
Accounts Payable 31 December 2016	10 000

Number of business days = 340.

6 What is the accounts receivable days for the partnership?

(A) 14 days   (A)

(B) 21 days   (B)

(C) 57 days   (C)

(D) 85 days   (D)

7 What is the accounts payable days for the partnership?

(A) 14 days   Ⓐ

(B) 21 days   Ⓑ

(C) 43 days   Ⓒ

(D) 64 days   Ⓓ

Liquidity ratios

8 The ratio that measures the firm's ability to cover its short-term obligations is called the

(A) Acid Test   Ⓐ

(B) Quick Ratio   Ⓑ

(C) Liquidity Ratio   Ⓒ

(D) Current Ratio.   Ⓓ

9 The ratio that measures the firm's ability to pay its short-term creditors should they demand payment is called the

(A) Current Ratio   Ⓐ

(B) Quick Ratio   Ⓑ

(C) Liquidity Ratio   Ⓒ

(D) Return on Investment.   Ⓓ

The data in Table 2.3 refers to <u>items **10–11**</u>.

Woodpecker Corporation provided a list of its assets and liabilities as in Table 2.3.

Table 2.3

	$
Cash	14 000
Buildings	140 000
Accounts Payable	16 000
Inventory	15 000
Marketable securities	8000
Machinery	60 000
Note Payable (6 months)	15 000
Mortgage	84 000
Bank overdraft	6000
Accounts Receivables	30 000
Note Payable (5 years)	70 000
Motor vehicles	53 000

10 What is the corporation's current ratio?

(A) 1.51:1 Ⓐ

(B) 1.68:1 Ⓑ

(C) 1.81:1 Ⓒ

(D) 2.35:1 Ⓓ

11 What is the corporation's acid test ratio?

(A) 1.19:1 Ⓐ

(B) 1.41:1 Ⓑ

(C) 1.81:1 Ⓒ

(D) 3.24:1 Ⓓ

12 What can be concluded from the comparison of the quick ratios of Company A's 1.25:1 to Company B's 0.85:1?

(A) Company A has more quick assets than Company B.   (A)

(B) Company A and Company B have the same current liabilities.   (B)

(C) Company B is a smaller business than Company A.   (C)

(D) Company A can pay its short-term obligations more comfortably.   (D)

Profitability

13 An income statement which uses ratios in vertical analysis is also called a

(A) Common size income statement   (A)

(B) Statement of financial performance   (B)

(C) Statement of comprehensive income   (C)

(D) Comparative income statement.   (D)

The information below refers to items **15–17**.

Mucorapo Company supplied the extracts as in Table 2.4 from its income statement for the period ended 30 April 2019.

Table 2.4

	$
Sales	156 000
Sales returns and allowances	4000
Cost of sales	72 000
Operating expenses	30 000
Other expenses	12 000
Other revenues	7000

Corporation Tax rate = 15%

14 What is the value of the gross profit percentage/gross margin?

(A) 22.80%   (A)

(B) 32.89%   (B)

(C) 51.28%   (C)

(D) 52.63%   (D)

15 What is the percentage of cost of sales to net sales?

(A) 47.37% (A)

(B) 48.72% (B)

(C) 67.11% (C)

(D) 77.22% (D)

16 What is the net profit percentage/net margin?

(A) 24.52% (A)

(B) 25.16% (B)

(C) 28.85% (C)

(D) 29.60% (D)

The information below refers to <u>items **17–19**</u>.

Belize Company provided the information in Table 2.5 from its current financial statements of 2017 and comparative data from 2016.

Table 2.5

	2017	2016
Net income	$75 000	$62 000
Retained profits b/f 1 January	$20 000	$25 000
Preference dividend	$6000	$6000
Ordinary dividends declared	$1.25 per share	$1.00 per share
Ordinary shares at $5.00 par	$130 000	$100 000
Market value per share	$25.00	$20.00

17 What is the income attributable to ordinary shareholders in 2016?

(A) $25 000 (A)

(B) $56 000 (B)

(C) $62 000 (C)

(D) $81 000 (D)

18 What is the value of earnings per share at the end of 2017?

(A) $2.65   (A)

(B) $2.88   (B)

(C) $3.00   (C)

(D) $3.26   (D)

19 What is the price earnings ratio for the company in 2017?

(A) 6.90   (A)

(B) 7.50   (B)

(C) 7.67   (C)

(D) 8.33   (D)

Solvency Ratios

The information below refers to items **20–22**

The information in Table 2.6 is from the financial statements of Negril Company and BlackRock Company for 2019.

Table 2.6

	Negril Company	BlackRock Company
Total current liabilities	$75 000	$115 000
Total non-current liabilities	$175 000	$185 000
Total assets	$500 000	$750 000
Total shareholders' equity	$250 000	$450 000

20 What is the debt to total assets ratio for BlackRock Company?

(A) 24.67%   (A)

(B) 40%   (B)

(C) 50%   (C)

(D) 60%   (D)

21 What is the debt to equity ratio for Negril Company?

(A) 0.67 times   Ⓐ

(B) 1 time   Ⓑ

(C) 1.67 times   Ⓒ

(D) 2 times   Ⓓ

22 It can be stated that Negril Company's debt to equity ratio is

(A) higher than that of BlackRock Company   Ⓐ

(B) lower than that of BlackRock Company   Ⓑ

(C) the same as that of BlackRock Company   Ⓒ

(D) showing better solvency than BlackRock Company.   Ⓓ

23 Which of the following statements identify the limitations of ratio analysis?

    I Different firms may use different accounting policies.

    II The use of historical data may not match the changes in the environment.

    III The profit for the year for business cannot be expressed in percentage terms.

(A) I and II   Ⓐ

(B) I and III   Ⓑ

(C) II and III   Ⓒ

(D) I, II and III   Ⓓ

1.3.3 Disclosures and Receivership

Inflation in accounting

1 When assets are valued at the present cost to replace them rather than their original acquisition price in the financial statements, this is called

(A) Present cost accounting   Ⓐ

(B) Historical cost accounting   Ⓑ

(C) Current cost accounting   Ⓒ

(D) Accrual cost accounting.   Ⓓ

Disclosures

2 The IAS that deals with provisions, contingent liabilities and contingent assets is

(A) IAS 1　　　　　　　　　　　　　　　　　　　　　　　Ⓐ

(B) IAS 2　　　　　　　　　　　　　　　　　　　　　　　Ⓑ

(C) IAS 10　　　　　　　　　　　　　　　　　　　　　　Ⓒ

(D) IAS 37.　　　　　　　　　　　　　　　　　　　　　Ⓓ

3 A liability of uncertain timing that is a present obligation that has arisen as a result of a past event which is probable and the amount can be reliably estimated is called a

(A) Current asset　　　　　　　　　　　　　　　　　　Ⓐ

(B) Provision　　　　　　　　　　　　　　　　　　　　Ⓑ

(C) Contingent liability　　　　　　　　　　　　　　　Ⓒ

(D) Non-current liability.　　　　　　　　　　　　　　Ⓓ

4 Which of the following items are considered one-off provisions?

　　I Settlement of a lawsuit

　　II Environmental clean-up cost

　　III Customer warranties or refunds

(A) I and II　　　　　　　　　　　　　　　　　　　　　Ⓐ

(B) I and III　　　　　　　　　　　　　　　　　　　　Ⓑ

(C) II and III　　　　　　　　　　　　　　　　　　　　Ⓒ

(D) I, II and III　　　　　　　　　　　　　　　　　　　Ⓓ

5 If the expenditure for a provision is to be covered by a third party and it is virtually certain that payment will be received if that third party settles the obligation then

(A) Do not record the provision anywhere.　　　　　　Ⓐ

(B) Record the information in the notes.　　　　　　　Ⓑ

(C) Record the reimbursement as a separate asset.　　Ⓒ

(D) Keep the information to announce at the AGM.　　Ⓓ

6 An event that creates a legal or constructive demand on the organisation's cash resources and results in the entity having no realistic alternative but to settle it is called

(A) an obligating event   Ⓐ

(B) a concerned event   Ⓑ

(C) a business event   Ⓒ

(D) a provision event.   Ⓓ

7 In measuring a provision under IAS 37, future events should be considered as follows

    I Review possible changes in applying existing technology.

    II Ignore possible gains on sales of assets.

    III Changes in exchange rates to provide best estimate of any present obligation.

(A) I and II   Ⓐ

(B) I and III   Ⓑ

(C) II and III   Ⓒ

(D) I, II and III   Ⓓ

The following information relates to <u>item **8**</u>.

Frank's Furniture Store allows its customers a 30-day return for refund policy. The store deducts a 10% restocking fee as required by law. The data in Table 3.1 about sales is provided.

Table 3.1

20 January 2017	$10 000
29 January 2017	$4000
27 February 2017	$7000
20 February 2017	$9000

8 What is the value of the provision to be recorded for February 2017, if any?

(A) Nothing   Ⓐ

(B) $14 400   Ⓑ

(C) $18 000   Ⓒ

(D) $27 000   Ⓓ

Contingent liabilities

9 Which of the following phrases are required to consider an item a contingent liability?

    I Must be reliably estimated

    II Must be a possible obligation

    III Cannot be reliably estimated

(A) I and II   Ⓐ

(B) I and III   Ⓑ

(C) II and III   Ⓒ

(D) I, II and III   Ⓓ

10 Under which of the following circumstances is a provision NOT recognised?

(A) Bonus plans for employees   Ⓐ

(B) Vacation pay for employees   Ⓑ

(C) Board decision for future expense   Ⓒ

(D) Warranties on goods sold   Ⓓ

11 What is the nature of a future event that is recorded as an expense and liability?

(A) The event is remote.   Ⓐ

(B) It is reasonably possible.   Ⓑ

(C) It is probable and can be reasonably estimated.   Ⓒ

(D) It is probable but cannot be reasonably estimated.   Ⓓ

12 Barbice Company has a policy of 2% warranty on sales. Its warranty payable account at 31 December 2019 was $1500. During the year 2020 the company's sales were $160 000 and it paid out $2100 in warranty commitments. What was the closing balance for the warranty account?

(A) $2100   Ⓐ

(B) $2600   Ⓑ

(C) $3200   Ⓒ

(D) $4700   Ⓓ

13 For a contingent liability not to be recorded, the event must be

(A) remote   (A)

(B) probable   (B)

(C) reasonably possible   (C)

(D) past.   (D)

14 For a contingent asset **not** to be disclosed in the notes to the accounts the event must be

    I remote

    II probable

    III reasonably possible.

(A) I or II   (A)

(B) I or III   (B)

(C) II or III   (C)

(D) I, II or III   (D)

Post Balance Sheet Events

15 Which of the following are post balance sheet events?

    I Determination of net realisable value of inventory

    II Discovery of errors that show that the financial statements are incorrect

    III Insolvency of a debtor before the financial statements are approved

(A) I and II   (A)

(B) I and III   (B)

(C) II and III   (C)

(D) I, II and III   (D)

16 Which IAS provides guidelines for the treatment of events after the reporting period?

(A) IAS 1   (A)

(B) IAS 2   (B)

(C) IAS 10   (C)

(D) IAS 37   (D)

17 Which of the following is a non-adjusting event?

(A) Insolvency of a debtor (A)

(B) Discovery of financial statement errors (B)

(C) Determination of net realisable value of inventory (C)

(D) Losses of inventory by fire (D)

18 Which event after the balance sheet date is an adjusting event?

(A) Acquisition of another business (A)

(B) Losses on fixed assets due to flood (B)

(C) Financial statements errors due to fraud (C)

(D) An issue of two shares for every one held (D)

19 A post balance sheet event must be a material event that occurs between the balance sheet date and the date that

(A) management have completed the financial statements (A)

(B) the financial statements are approved by the Board of Directors (B)

(C) external auditors have finished checking the financial statements (C)

(D) the Annual General Meeting (AGM) occurs with the shareholders. (D)

Other disclosure notes

20 Which is not a financial statement?

(A) Balance sheet (A)

(B) Income Statement (B)

(C) Trial Balance (C)

(D) Cashflow Statement (D)

21 The balance sheet is also known as the

(A) Statement of Retained Earnings (A)

(B) Statement of Financial Position (B)

(C) Statement of Changes in Equity (C)

(D) Statement of Changes in Financial Position. (D)

22 According to IAS 1 (IFRS for SMEs 5.11), an entity shall present the analysis of expenses using a classification based on the

(A) function of the expenses (A)

(B) age of the expenses (B)

(C) amount of the expenses (C)

(D) alphabetical order of expenses. (D)

23 Under IAS 1, which item is not a disclosure of the statement of financial position?

(A) Property, Plant and Equipment (A)

(B) Inventories (B)

(C) Provisions (C)

(D) Expenses. (D)

24 According to IAS 1 (IFRS for SMEs 8.4), which is the correct order for presenting notes to the financial statements?

    I Summary of significant accounting policies applied

    II Any other disclosures

    III Statement of compliance with IFRS for SMEs or IASs

    IV Sequentially ordered supporting information for financial statement items

(A) I, II, III and IV (A)

(B) I, III, IV and II (B)

(C) III, I, IV and II (C)

(D) III, IV, I and II (D)

Receivership

25 Which is not a reason that a business may result in bankruptcy?

(A) Loss of key employees   Ⓐ

(B) Loss of a shareholder   Ⓑ

(C) Fire in the firm   Ⓒ

(D) Fraudulent activity   Ⓓ

The following information about eight steps in the receivership process refers to items **26–28**:

1. (i)

2. Creditor petitions court for receiving order.

3. If approved, Court appoints a receiver.

4. (ii)

5. Receiver takes custody of assets.

6. (iii)

7. Commercially dispose of unwanted assets and assess creditors' claims.

8. (iv)

26 What does (i) represent?

(A) Receiver notifies the debtors and creditors of his/her appointment.   Ⓐ

(B) Receiver prepares a monthly business performance statement.   Ⓑ

(C) Receiver makes a determination that an act of bankruptcy was committed.   Ⓒ

(D) Receiver opens a bank account in his/her name.   Ⓓ

27 What does (ii) represent?

(A) Receiver notifies the debtors and creditors of his/her appointment.   Ⓐ

(B) Receiver prepares a monthly business performance statement.   Ⓑ

(C) Receiver makes a determination that an act of bankruptcy was committed.   Ⓒ

(D) Receiver opens a bank account in his/her name.   Ⓓ

28 What does (iv) represent?

    (A) Receiver notifies the debtors and creditors of his/her appointment.   Ⓐ

    (B) Receiver prepares a monthly business performance statement.   Ⓑ

    (C) Receiver makes a determination that an act of bankruptcy was committed.   Ⓒ

    (D) Receiver opens a bank account in his/her name.   Ⓓ

29 Eleanor, a sole trader, has used her house as collateral to secure a mortgage of $173 000. The loan is

    (A) a secured claim   Ⓐ

    (B) a partly secured claim   Ⓑ

    (C) an unsecured claim   Ⓒ

    (D) An illegal claim.   Ⓓ

30 Expenses payable are considered

    (A) secured claims   Ⓐ

    (B) partly secured claims   Ⓑ

    (C) unsecured claims   Ⓒ

    (D) illegal claims.   Ⓓ

Unit 2: Cost and Management Accounting

1 Cost and management accounting

    I assists in identifying unprofitable products or services

    II provides reports showing the cost of producing goods or services

    III assists in calculating the selling price of products and services.

(A) I   Ⓐ

(B) II   Ⓑ

(C) III   Ⓒ

(D) I, II and III   Ⓓ

2 Cost accounting involves

    I identifying product costs

    II measuring product costs

    III recording and reporting of product costs.

(A) I   Ⓐ

(B) II   Ⓑ

(C) I and III   Ⓒ

(D) I, II and III   Ⓓ

3 Managerial accounting provides information

    I to meet internal users' needs

    II to help creditors make economic decisions

    III for focusing on the future.

(A) I   Ⓐ

(B) II   Ⓑ

(C) I and III   Ⓒ

(D) II and III   Ⓓ

4 Which of the following types of accounting is regulated by preparing financial statements in accordance with Generally Accepted Accounting Principles (GAAP)?

(A) Cost accounting   Ⓐ

(B) Social accounting   Ⓑ

(C) Financial accounting   Ⓒ

(D) Managerial accounting   Ⓓ

5 Management Accounting emphasises that data should be

    I relevant

    II objective

    III flexible.

(A) I   Ⓐ

(B) II   Ⓑ

(C) I and II   Ⓒ

(D) I and III   Ⓓ

2.1.2 Manufacturing Accounts Preparation

1 A manufacturing statement

(A) reports operating income made for the period   Ⓐ

(B) computes cost of goods manufactured for the period   Ⓑ

(C) computes cost of goods sold for the period   Ⓒ

(D) reports operating expenses made for the period.   Ⓓ

2 The elements of prime costs are

      I overhead cost

      II direct labour

      III direct material.

(A) I   Ⓐ

(B) II   Ⓑ

(C) I and II   Ⓒ

(D) II and III   Ⓓ

3 Which of the following inventories distinguishes a merchandising company's Statement of Financial Position from that of a manufacturing company?

      I Raw materials

      II Work in process

      III Finished goods

(A) I   Ⓐ

(B) II   Ⓑ

(C) I and II   Ⓒ

(D) I, II and III   Ⓓ

4 Which of the following computations for cost of goods sold is correct?

(A) Beginning work in process + cost of goods manufactured – ending work in process   Ⓐ

(B) Beginning raw materials inventory + cost of goods manufactured – ending raw materials inventory   Ⓑ

(C) Beginning finished goods inventory – cost of goods manufactured + ending finished goods inventory   Ⓒ

(D) Beginning finished goods inventory + cost of goods manufactured – ending finished goods inventory   Ⓓ

The information listed below refers to <u>item 5</u>.

Imani Harry provided the information shown in Table 2.1.

Table 2.1

Cost of goods manufactured	$800 000
Beginning finished goods inventory	$100 000
Ending finished goods inventory	$300 000

5 The total of cost of goods sold is

(A) $400 000

(B) $600 000

(C) $800 000

(D) $900 000.

Ⓐ

Ⓑ

Ⓒ

Ⓓ

2.1.3 Cost Classification and Curves

1 Which of the following costs would NOT be considered as marketing and selling costs?

(A) Advertising

(B) Sales salaries

(C) Sales commission

(D) Executive compensation

Ⓐ

Ⓑ

Ⓒ

Ⓓ

2 Manufacturing costs are also called

    I non-inventoriable

    II product cost

    III inventoriable.

(A) I

(B) II

(C) I and II

(D) II and III

Ⓐ

Ⓑ

Ⓒ

Ⓓ

Items **3–4** refer to the information shown in figure 3.1.

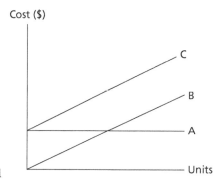

Figure 3.1

3 What cost is represented by A in Figure 3.1?

(A) Fixed cost   (A)

(B) Mixed cost   (B)

(C) Variable cost   (C)

(D) Semi-variable cost   (D)

4 What cost does B represent in the cost diagram shown in Figure 3.1?

(A) Fixed cost   (A)

(B) Mixed cost   (B)

(C) Variable cost   (C)

(D) Semi-variable cost   (D)

5 Costs such as rent and factory insurance are considered as

    I controllable costs

    II uncontrollable costs

    III cost behaviour.

(A) I   (A)

(B) II   (B)

(C) I and III   (C)

(D) I, II and III   (D)

Principles of material control and inventory control

Items **1–2** refer to the following information.

The elements of the material control process are shown in Figure 4.1.

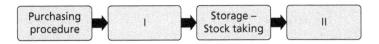

Figure 4.1

1 What feature of the inventory control diagram does 'I' represent in this process?

(A) Inspection of materials   Ⓐ

(B) Receipt of goods   Ⓑ

(C) Goods taken to stores   Ⓒ

(D) Issues of materials   Ⓓ

2 What feature of the inventory control diagram does 'II' represent in the above process?

(A) Receipt   Ⓐ

(B) Inspection of materials   Ⓑ

(C) Goods taken to stores   Ⓒ

(D) Issues   Ⓓ

3 Which one of the following would NOT be considered as direct materials for a roti shop?

(A) Oil   Ⓐ

(B) Dhall   Ⓑ

(C) Rice   Ⓒ

(D) Flour   Ⓓ

4 The formula to determine the purchases cost of inventory is

(A) prices only ⒜

(B) prices – sales discounts – shipping (freight charges) ⒝

(C) prices + sales discounts – shipping (freight charges) ⒞

(D) price – sales discounts + shipping (freight charges). ⒟

5 Which of the following departments issue materials to the production department?

(A) Sales ⒜

(B) Purchases ⒝

(C) Accounts ⒞

(D) Warehouse ⒟

6 The overall objective of inventory control is to minimise costs associated with stock. The category of carrying costs includes

    I storage charges

   II transport costs

  III material handling costs.

(A) I ⒜

(B) I and II ⒝

(C) I and III ⒞

(D) II and III ⒟

7 Which of the following stock allowances covers errors in forecasting the lead time or demand during the lead time?

(A) Safety stock (Minimum level) ⒜

(B) Economic Order Quantity (EOQ) ⒝

(C) Maximum level ⒞

(D) Reorder level ⒟

Item **8** refers to the information listed below.

Clyde supplied the information shown in Table 4.1 for the month of June.

Table 4.1

1 June	Inventory on hand 3000 units @ $8 each
8 June	Purchased 5000 units @ $8.40 each
14 June	Sold 4000 units @ $14.00 each
18 June	Purchased 6000 units for $8.00 each
25 June	Sold 7000 units for $14.00 each
30 June	Inventory on hand 3000 units

8 Using the Last in First out (LIFO) cost flow method, what is the value of closing inventory for the month of June for Clyde?

(A) $24 000   Ⓐ

(B) $24 600   Ⓑ

(C) $24 660   Ⓒ

(D) $32 400   Ⓓ

9 When costs are rising, which method gives a lower inventory figure in the Balance Sheet?

(A) Last In First Out (LIFO) method   Ⓐ

(B) First In First Out (FIFO) method   Ⓑ

(C) Average Cost (AVCO) Method   Ⓒ

(D) Next In First Out (NIFO) Method   Ⓓ

10 Cost classification for stock valuation may include

    I period and product costs

    II elements of manufacturing costs

    III job and process costs.

(A) I   Ⓐ

(B) II   Ⓑ

(C) I and III   Ⓒ

(D) I, II and III   Ⓓ

11 Waste materials can be defined as

      I toxic

      II reactive

      III corrosive.

(A) I   Ⓐ

(B) II   Ⓑ

(C) I and II   Ⓒ

(D) I, II and III   Ⓓ

12 An item that costs $60 has an annual carrying cost of $3 per unit. The ordering cost is $20 per order and the annual average of the items is 30 000 units. What is the economic order quantity?

(A) 100 units   Ⓐ

(B) 173 units   Ⓑ

(C) 633 units   Ⓒ

(D) 1095 units   Ⓓ

13 The assumptions of EOQ are

      I The demand rate is uniform and known.

      II The order is not delivered at the same time.

      III The item cost does vary with the order size.

(A) I   Ⓐ

(B) II   Ⓑ

(C) I and II   Ⓒ

(D) II and III   Ⓓ

14 Reorder point is determined by

    I daily usage

    II lead time

    III safety stock.

(**A**) I   Ⓐ

(**B**) II   Ⓑ

(**C**) I and III   Ⓒ

(**D**) I, II and III   Ⓓ

The information in Table 4.2 refers to <u>item **15**</u>.

Table 4.2

Lead time	3 weeks
Average weekly usage	100 units
Maximum weekly usage	150 units
Safety stock	70 units

15 The reorder point is

(**A**) 100 units   Ⓐ

(**B**) 150 units   Ⓑ

(**C**) 300 units   Ⓒ

(**D**) 450 units.   Ⓓ

1 Which of these labour costs are treated in MOST instances as manufacturing overheads?

    I Idle time

    II Direct labour

    III Labour fringe benefits

(**A**) I   Ⓐ

(**B**) I and II   Ⓑ

(**C**) I and III   Ⓒ

(**D**) II and III   Ⓓ

2 Which of the following employee remunerations will result in indirect labour costs?

    I Janitors

    II Supervisors

    III Carpenters

(**A**) I   Ⓐ

(**B**) II   Ⓑ

(**C**) I and II   Ⓒ

(**D**) II and III   Ⓓ

Items **3–4** refer to the information noted below.

Frank earns $18.00 per hour weekly. He normally works 40 hours per week. For one week, he was idle for 3 hours due to materials shortage.

3 The direct labour is

(**A**) $666   Ⓐ

(**B**) $720   Ⓑ

(**C**) $774   Ⓒ

(**D**) $828.   Ⓓ

4 Frank's total wages is

(A) $666   Ⓐ

(B) $720   Ⓑ

(C) $774   Ⓒ

(D) $828.   Ⓓ

Technological changes (advances)

5 A company replaced its labour force with automated equipment. The benefits of the change may

    I cause a decrease in labour costs

    II reduce defective outputs

    III offer greater speed, consistency, reliability and flexibility.

(A) I   Ⓐ

(B) II   Ⓑ

(C) I and II   Ⓒ

(D) I, II and III   Ⓓ

6 Wages paid to assembly line workers are classified as

(A) direct labour   Ⓐ

(B) direct materials   Ⓑ

(C) manufacturing overhead costs   Ⓒ

(D) merchandising overhead costs.   Ⓓ

7 An employer's contribution to National Insurance, Social Security and Pension Fund for production workers are recorded as

     I manufacturing overhead

     II direct labour

     III period cost.

(**A**) I   Ⓐ

(**B**) II   Ⓑ

(**C**) I or II   Ⓒ

(**D**) II or III   Ⓓ

8 When a customer makes a direct request for workers to complete a job in a timely manner, the overtime is charged as

(**A**) overhead costs   Ⓐ

(**B**) direct costs   Ⓑ

(**C**) idle time   Ⓒ

(**D**) commission.   Ⓓ

9 A payment system where employees are paid a fixed amount for each unit of production is known as

(**A**) piece work   Ⓐ

(**B**) commission   Ⓑ

(**C**) bonus   Ⓒ

(**D**) basic pay.   Ⓓ

10 Kirk Company pays its production employees $0.50 for every completed unit produced from 0 to 500 units and $0.75 for every completed unit produced in excess of 500 units. This method of remuneration is best described as

(A) straight piece rate ⒶⒶ

(B) guaranteed day rate ⒷⒷ

(C) differential piece rates ⒸⒸ

(D) premium bonus. ⒹⒹ

Items **11–12** refer to the information noted below.

Joyce earns $50 per hour in an assembly plant. She is paid time and half overtime in excess of 40 hours working time. During the week Joyce works 80 hours and has no idle time.

11 The total direct labour is

(A) $1000 Ⓐ

(B) $2000 Ⓑ

(C) $4000 Ⓒ

(D) $4500. Ⓓ

12 The total manufacturing overhead cost is

(A) $1000 Ⓐ

(B) $2000 Ⓑ

(C) $3000 Ⓒ

(D) $4500. Ⓓ

13 In most Caribbean countries, labour fringe benefits are paid by employers. These costs include

     I Overtime premium

     II Retirement plans

     III National Insurance Schemes (Social Security).

(A) I   Ⓐ

(B) II   Ⓑ

(C) I and III   Ⓒ

(D) II and III   Ⓓ

Item **14** refers to the information below.

Eartha is paid by differential piecework and rates have been agreed as in the Table 5.1.

Table 5.1

Up to 600 units	$0.50 per unit
601–700 units	$0.55 per unit
701–800 units	$0.60 per unit
801 and above	$0.65

Eartha produced 745 good units.

14 The total amount of Eartha's wages is

(A) $300   Ⓐ

(B) $382   Ⓑ

(C) $385   Ⓒ

(D) $412.   Ⓓ

15 Commission is paid to workers

   I as a fixed percentage

   II as a rate based on unit of product

   III when a worker performs a task less than the allowed time.

(A) I

(B) I and II

(C) I and III

(D) II and III

(A)

(B)

(C)

(D)

2.1.6 Elements of Cost: Overheads

<u>Item **1**</u> refers to the following information.

Kirky Stores Limited allocates its janitorial services among three departments according to the floor space occupied. The total of the janitorial services is $28 000 and the amount of floor space occupied is shown in Table 6.1.

Table 6.1

Food department	250 square metres
Men's clothing department	150 square metres
Household department	500 square metres
Total space occupied	1000 square metres

1 The department share of the costs of janitorial services for the Household department is

(A) $4200

(B) $7000

(C) $9800

(D) $14 000.

(A)

(B)

(C)

(D)

Item 2 refers to the following information.

Akouswa has two service departments; Personnel and Janitorial. Her operating departments are Mixing and Baking. The data for the current year appears in Table 6.2.

Table 6.2

	Service		Operating	
	Personnel	**Janitorial**	**Mixing**	**Baking**
Overhead costs	$800 000	$500 000	$1 000 000	$2 000 000
Employees	20	10	50	80
Space occupied thousand square feet	30	20	60	100

Additional information:

- Personnel department costs are allocated on the basis of employees.
- Janitorial costs are allocated on the basis of space occupied.
- The company makes no distinction between fixed and variable costs in its service department allocation.

2 If the step down method of service department allocation is used and the Personnel department costs are allocated first, how much Personnel department cost would be allocated to the Janitorial department?

(A) $35 714   Ⓐ

(B) $50 000   Ⓑ

(C) $53 333   Ⓒ

(D) $57 142   Ⓓ

3 Which of the following bases are NOT usually recommended to be commonly used as an appropriate share of a firm's total overhead?

(A) Direct labour hours   Ⓐ

(B) Machine hours   Ⓑ

(C) Direct labour costs   Ⓒ

(D) Prime costs   Ⓓ

4 Which of the following methods for allocating service department costs will go directly to a firm's production or operating department?

(A) Direct method   Ⓐ

(B) Stepped down method   Ⓑ

(C) Repeated distribution method   Ⓒ

(D) Simultaneous equation method   Ⓓ

5 For which of the following costs would it be appropriate to use floor area or volume as a basis of apportionment?

(A) Rent expense   Ⓐ

(B) Canteen cost   Ⓑ

(C) Storekeeping cost   Ⓒ

(D) Personnel department cost   Ⓓ

Item **6** refers to the information given in Table 6.3.

Table 6.3

Actual direct labour hours worked	15 000
Actual overhead cost	$540 000
Budgeted direct labour hours	20 000
Budgeted overhead cost	$550 000

6 The overhead absorption rate based on direct labour hours is

(A) $27.00   Ⓐ

(B) $27.50   Ⓑ

(C) $36.00   Ⓒ

(D) $36.67.   Ⓓ

7 Manufacturing overhead includes

    I indirect materials

    II indirect labour

    III direct materials.

(A) I   Ⓐ

(B) II   Ⓑ

(C) I and II   Ⓒ

(D) I and III   Ⓓ

8 Manufacturing overhead is also known as

    I factory overhead

    II factory burden

    III indirect manufacturing costs.

(A) I   Ⓐ

(B) II   Ⓑ

(C) I and II   Ⓒ

(D) I, II and III   Ⓓ

9 A cost centre is considered as a

    I location or department

    II function

    III somewhere used to accumulate costs.

(A) I   Ⓐ

(B) II   Ⓑ

(C) I and II   Ⓒ

(D) I, II and III   Ⓓ

10 The principle or method used to spread cost over cost centres is known as

(A) allocation   Ⓐ

(B) apportionment   Ⓑ

(C) overhead applied   Ⓒ

(D) overhead absorption.   Ⓓ

11 The process used to charge overhead in suitable proportions to individual jobs is known as

    I overhead absorption

    II apportionment

    III allocation.

(A) I   Ⓐ

(B) II   Ⓑ

(C) I and II   Ⓒ

(D) II and III   Ⓓ

12 Which of the following overhead bases would be most appropriate to be used for costs such as depreciation on machinery?

(A) Prime cost   Ⓐ

(B) Labour cost   Ⓑ

(C) Labour hours   Ⓒ

(D) Machine hours   Ⓓ

Items **13–14** refer to the information below.

Job ABC is made up by two cost centres: Assembly and Finishing Departments. The overhead absorption rates for the departments are $8.00 and $15.00 per labour hours respectively. The job details are as in Table 6.4.

Table 6.4

	Assembly	Finishing
Direct labour	8 hours × $5 = $40	15 hours × $6 = $90
Direct material	$130	$35

13 The total overhead is

(A) $64   Ⓐ

(B) $225   Ⓑ

(C) $289   Ⓒ

(D) $584.   Ⓓ

14 The total production cost is

(A) $225   Ⓐ

(B) $289   Ⓑ

(C) $295   Ⓒ

(D) $584.   Ⓓ

15 Over absorption (application) is charged, based on production, when applied overhead is

     I greater than actual overhead

    II less than actual overhead

   III equal to actual overhead.

(A) I   Ⓐ

(B) II   Ⓑ

(C) I and III   Ⓒ

(D) II and III   Ⓓ

Items 1–2 refer to the information below.

A Company receives a special order for 200 units. This order yields an additional fixed cost of $400 to its normal costs. Without the order, the company is operating at 75% capacity and produces 7500 units of products at the costs as shown in Table 7.1.

Table 7.1

Direct material	$37 500
Direct labour	$60 000
Overheads (30% variable)	$20 000
Selling expenses (60% variable)	$25 000

The special order will not affect normal unit sales and will not increase fixed overheads and selling expenses. Variable selling expenses on the special order are reduced to one-half the normal amount.

1 The cost to produce the special order is

(A) $3160

(B) $3360

(C) $4160

(D) $4360.

Ⓐ Ⓑ Ⓒ Ⓓ

2 The price per unit to earn $1000 on this order is

(A) $14.80

(B) $15.80

(C) $20.80

(D) $21.80.

Ⓐ Ⓑ Ⓒ Ⓓ

3 Which of the following costs are applicable to decision making?

(A) Sunk costs   Ⓐ

(B) Relevant costs   Ⓑ

(C) Opportunity costs   Ⓒ

(D) Irrelevant costs   Ⓓ

<u>Item 4</u> refers to the following information.

Priya Cap must decide whether to make or buy school uniforms. The costs of producing 75 000 uniforms for schools are as shown in Table 7.2.

Table 7.2

Direct materials	$80 000
Direct labour	$40 000
Variable manufacturing overhead	$10 000
Factory overhead	$5000
Total	$135 000

Additional information that may affect the decision is that instead of making the uniforms at an average price of $1.80 ($135 000 ÷ 75 000), the company has the opportunity to outsource the making of school uniforms at $1.50. If the uniforms are purchased, all the variable costs and one-half of fixed costs will be eliminated.

4 The net income increase (decrease) is

(A) ($20 000)   Ⓐ

(B) $20 000   Ⓑ

(C) ($22 500)   Ⓒ

(D) $22 500.   Ⓓ

5 The costs that are not considered in decision making are

    I cost behaviour

    II sunk cost and opportunity cost

    III marginal and incremental cost.

(A) I   Ⓐ

(B) II   Ⓑ

(C) I and II   Ⓒ

(D) I, II and III   Ⓓ

6 The potential benefit given up when selecting one course of action over another action is known as

(A) sunk cost   Ⓐ

(B) discretionary cost   Ⓑ

(C) irrelevant cost   Ⓒ

(D) opportunity cost.   Ⓓ

7 Which of the following cost terms used in decision making reveals the difference between two alternatives?

(A) Sunk cost   Ⓐ

(B) Future cost   Ⓑ

(C) Differential cost   Ⓒ

(D) Opportunity cost   Ⓓ

8 An equipment NOT yet purchased may be considered as

      I sunk cost

      II relevant cost

      III opportunity cost.

(A) I   Ⓐ

(B) II   Ⓑ

(C) I and II   Ⓒ

(D) II and III   Ⓓ

9 Relevant costs are

      I future costs

      II differential costs

      III mixed costs.

(A) I   Ⓐ

(B) II   Ⓑ

(C) I and II   Ⓒ

(D) II and III   Ⓓ

10 The key non-financial (qualitative) factors considered in decision making are

      I psychological

      II social

      III environmental.

(A) I   Ⓐ

(B) II   Ⓑ

(C) I and II   Ⓒ

(D) I, II and III   Ⓓ

11 Short-term special decisions are known as

      I differential analysis

      II incremental analysis

      III break-even analysis.

(A) I   Ⓐ

(B) II   Ⓑ

(C) I and II   Ⓒ

(D) II and III   Ⓓ

Item **12** refers to the following information.

Tanya manufactures two products and provided the data in Table 7.3.

Table 7.3

	Total $	Product A $	Product B $
Sales revenue	200 000	100 000	100 000
Variable costs	(110 000)	(70 000)	(40 000)
Contribution margin	90 000	30 000	60 000
Fixed costs	(58 000)	(18 000)	(40 000)
Operating income	32 000	12 000	20 000

Assuming that Product B is discontinued, 50% of the fixed costs would be avoidable costs.

12 If Product B is discontinued, Tanya's operating income will

(A) decrease by $20 000   Ⓐ

(B) decrease by $40 000   Ⓑ

(C) decrease by $60 000   Ⓒ

(D) decrease by $100 000.   Ⓓ

13 Which of the following are NOT relevant for decision making?

(A) Costs already spent   (A)

(B) The cost of items bought on credit   (B)

(C) Costs which will change in the future   (C)

(D) Costs which do not vary significantly from budgets   (D)

Items **14–15** refer to the following information.

Twin Ice Delights makes tropical fruit ice cream. The company is considering buying the ice cream from a supplier rather than making it on its compound. The company makes an average of 500 local flavours of ice cream per year. Twin Ice Delight discloses that the costs of making its tropical fruit ice cream are as in Table 7.4.

Table 7.4

Direct materials	$2500
Direct labour	$1000
Variable manufacturing overhead	$200
Fixed manufacturing overhead	$1000
Total manufacturing cost	$4700

Cost per ice cream ($4700 ÷ 500) = $9.40.

Fixed costs include depreciation on equipment. Twin Ice expects to retain the equipment. The company can buy in the ice cream for $7.

14 The total variable cost for making the ice cream is

(A) $3500   (A)

(B) $3700   (B)

(C) $4700   (C)

(D) $7200.   (D)

15 The total differential cost is

(A) $200   (A)

(B) ($200)   (B)

(C) ($1200)   (C)

(D) $1200.   (D)

1 Traditional costing for applying overheads uses

    I total estimated overhead

    II departmental activity bases

    III plant-wide activity base.

(A) I and II   Ⓐ

(B) I and III   Ⓑ

(C) II and III   Ⓒ

(D) I, II and III   Ⓓ

2 In activity based costing, activity rates are determined by the use of

(A) total estimated overhead divided by a plant wide cost driver   Ⓐ

(B) total estimated overhead divided by individual cost drivers   Ⓑ

(C) individual overhead cost items divided by a plant-wide cost driver   Ⓒ

(D) individual overhead cost items divided by individual related cost drivers.   Ⓓ

3 When whole items of cost are charged directly to cost it is referred to as cost

(A) allocation   Ⓐ

(B) apportionment   Ⓑ

(C) absorption   Ⓒ

(D) allotment.   Ⓓ

4 The apportionment of rental cost for a building is best done on the basis of

(A) labour hours   Ⓐ

(B) machine hours   Ⓑ

(C) square footage   Ⓒ

(D) number of employees.   Ⓓ

5 The best suited apportionment base for maintenance cost of factory machines is

(A) labour hours   Ⓐ

(B) machine hours   Ⓑ

(C) square footage   Ⓒ

(D) number of employees.   Ⓓ

The following information refers to items **6–8**.

Marloy company manufactures two products, R1 and R2. The company uses the traditional method of absorbing overhead based on labour cost. It supplied the information shown in Table 1.1.

Table 1.1

	R1	**R2**
Labour hours per unit	2.5	3.5
Labour rate per unit ($9.00 per labour hour)	$22.50	$31.50
Number of units produced	4000	6000

Marloy's total estimated overhead cost is $250 000.

6 The total labour hours for producing all of R1 units is

(A) 10 000   Ⓐ

(B) 14 000   Ⓑ

(C) 15 000   Ⓒ

(D) 21 000.   Ⓓ

7 What is the value of predetermined overhead absorption rate (POHAR)?

(A) $0.90 per direct labour hour   Ⓐ

(B) $0.90 per direct labour dollar   Ⓑ

(C) $8.06 per direct labour hour   Ⓒ

(D) $8.06 direct labour dollar   Ⓓ

8 The total labour cost for producing R1 is

(A) $36 000   Ⓐ

(B) $54 000   Ⓑ

(C) $90 000   Ⓒ

(D) $135 000.   Ⓓ

The information below is relevant for <u>items 9–11</u>.

The data in Table 1.2 obtains to the Zelnik company for the year 2016.

Table 1.2

	Overhead costs $	Activity
Repair and maintenance	44 000	10 000 machine hours
Rent	126 000	7000 square feet
Electricity	65 000	5000 kilowatt hours
Telephones	46 000	1150 phone calls
Total overhead cost	281 000	

9 Using traditional costing, what is the predetermined overhead absorption rate if the company uses machine hours as its base?

(A) $4.40   Ⓐ

(B) $13.00   Ⓑ

(C) $18.00   Ⓒ

(D) $28.10   Ⓓ

10 If the company uses ABC, what is the overhead absorption rate for Telephones?

(A) $4.40   Ⓐ

(B) $13.00   Ⓑ

(C) $18.00   Ⓒ

(D) $40.00   Ⓓ

11 If the company uses ABC, what is the overhead absorption rate for Rent?

(A) $4.40   Ⓐ

(B) $13.00   Ⓑ

(C) $18.00   Ⓒ

(D) $40.00   Ⓓ

The information below is relevant for <u>items **12–15**</u>.

Sparkles Inc. manufactures two tablets, Custom and Slimline, and provided the information given in Table 1.3.

Table 1.3

	Cost $	Activity base
Set-ups	171 000	Number of set-ups
Machine maintenance	81 000	Number of machine hours
Total manufacturing overhead costs	252 000	

Additional information is presented in Table 1.4.

Table 1.4

	Slimline	Custom
Direct labour hours	4200	10 800
Number of set-ups	180	120
Number of machine hours	5400	3600
Number of units	225	450

The company uses the traditional method of allocating overhead based on direct labour hours but the new accountant has advised the use of ABC.

12 What is the predetermined overhead absorption rate for Sparkles Inc.?

(A) $5.40   Ⓐ

(B) $11.40   Ⓑ

(C) $16.80   Ⓒ

(D) $58.30   Ⓓ

13 What is the value of overhead absorbed for the Slimline tablets under the traditional costing method?

(A) $60 480   Ⓐ

(B) $70 560   Ⓑ

(C) $90 720   Ⓒ

(D) $181 440   Ⓓ

14 What is the value of overhead absorbed for the Custom tablets under the ABC method?

(A) $100 800   Ⓐ

(B) $117 000   Ⓑ

(C) $135 000   Ⓒ

(D) $151 200   Ⓓ

15 What is the difference in overhead cost absorbed between the traditional and ABC methods for the Slimline tablets?

(A) $30 240   Ⓐ

(B) $46 440   Ⓑ

(C) $64 440   Ⓒ

(D) $80 640   Ⓓ

1 The costing system commonly used for costing products that are unique, identifiable and distinct from each other is called

(A) Absorption costing ⒜

(B) Job costing ⒝

(C) Marginal costing ⒞

(D) Process costing. ⒟

The following information is relevant for items **2–4**.

Paul Stone, a sole trader, makes custom furniture. At the beginning of April 2017, Jobs 417 and 418 were in progress. Jobs 419, 420, 421, 422, 423 and 424 were started during the month of April 2017. Jobs 421, 423 and 424 were incomplete at the end of April 2017. At the end of April 2017 Jobs 417, 418, 420 and 422 were sold.

2 How many jobs were complete at the end of April 2017?

(A) 1 ⒜

(B) 3 ⒝

(C) 4 ⒞

(D) 5 ⒟

3 How many jobs were in finished goods inventory at the end of April 2017?

(A) 1 ⒜

(B) 3 ⒝

(C) 4 ⒞

(D) 5 ⒟

4 The number of jobs sold at the end of April 2017 is

(A) 1 ⒜

(B) 3 ⒝

(C) 4 ⒞

(D) 5. ⒟

The following information is relevant for items **5–6**.

Greenidge Art, painters of commissioned pieces, supplied the following information for the year with respect to direct labour. The company's predetermined overhead absorption rate (POHAR) is 60% of direct labour cost.

Total estimated direct labour cost for the year	$3 600 000
Total estimated direct labour hours	30 000 hours

The following information was supplied for Jobs 119 and 121.

Job	119	121
Direct materials	$4000	$6000
Direct labour hours	28	32

5 What is the overhead applied to Job 119?

(A) $2016

(B) $2304

(C) $3360

(D) $3840

6 What is the selling price for Job 121 if Greenidge Art uses a 10% mark up?

(A) $9376.00

(B) $10 313.60

(C) $12 144.00

(D) $13 358.40

7 Which business is most likely to use a job costing system?

(A) Car production

(B) Taxi service

(C) Soft drink bottling

(D) Oil refinery

8 Which business type will not use job costing?

(A) Bridge building (A)

(B) Sign painting (B)

(C) Custom furniture manufacture (C)

(D) Sugar refinery (D)

9 Job P123 for Prudent Landscapers has direct labour cost and direct materials cost of $25 000 and $5000 respectively. What is the overhead application rate if the job costs totalled $34 000 and overhead is applied on the basis of direct labour cost?

(A) 13% (A)

(B) 15% (B)

(C) 16% (C)

(D) 80% (D)

10 Suzanne provides interior decorating for residential properties. Job 2X34 consisted of 32 professional hours at a rate of $250 per hour. Her direct materials costs were $6000. If the total cost of the job was $16 800, the overhead application rate based on direct costs was

(A) 17% (A)

(B) 20% (B)

(C) 35% (C)

(D) 47%. (D)

The following information is relevant for <u>items 11–14</u>.

Kay Enterprises, makers of specialty cakes, supplied the information in Table 2.1.

Table 2.1

Job No.	Opening work in process ($)	Direct materials ($)	Direct labour ($)
617	120	100	120
618	200	–	130
619	–	250	300
620	–	100	240
621	–	420	250
622	–	360	230
623	–	390	260

Overhead is applied at a rate of 120% of labour costs. Jobs 620 and 623 were incomplete at the end of the period and Jobs 619 and 622 remained finished goods inventory.

11 What is the total overhead applied for the period?

(A) $1536 Ⓐ

(B) $1824 Ⓑ

(C) $1836 Ⓒ

(D) $1944 Ⓓ

12 What is the value of ending work in process inventory?

(A) $1494 Ⓐ

(B) $1590 Ⓑ

(C) $1776 Ⓒ

(D) $1872 Ⓓ

13 What is the value of cost of goods sold?

    (A) $1340   (A)

    (B) $1836   (B)

    (C) $1932   (C)

    (D) $1940   (D)

14 If the business uses a 10% mark-up on cost, the value of sales for the period would be

    (A) $1474.00   (A)

    (B) $2019.60   (B)

    (C) $2125.20   (C)

    (D) $2134.00.   (D)

15 Total under-applied overhead occurs when

    (A) applied overhead is greater than actual overhead   (A)

    (B) actual overhead is greater than applied overhead   (B)

    (C) estimated overhead is greater than applied overhead   (C)

    (D) applied overhead is greater than estimated overhead.   (D)

The following information is relevant for <u>items **16–17**</u>.

Gaines Designs, an architecture business, uses a predetermined overhead rate of 75% of direct labour costs. Job 193 incurred labour cost of $240 000, of which $200 000 was direct and the remainder indirect. Actual overhead incurred was $175 000 inclusive of indirect labour cost.

16 The amount of overhead applied to the job was

    (A) $131 250   (A)

    (B) $150 000   (B)

    (C) $161 250   (C)

    (D) $180 000.   (D)

17 How much was the over/under applied overhead to Job 193?

(A) $25 000 over-applied   Ⓐ

(B) $25 000 under-applied   Ⓑ

(C) $65 000 over-applied   Ⓒ

(D) $65 000 under-applied   Ⓓ

The following information is relevant for <u>items **18–20**</u>.

Nichols Construction has two jobs in July, Jobs N75 and N76. Overhead is applied at a rate of $25.00 per labour hour. The cost information in Table 2.2 was supplied.

Table 2.2

Job	N75	N76
Direct Materials	$66 000	$24 200
Direct Labour cost	$84 000	$37 800
Direct Labour hours	4000	1800

Actual overhead costs for the month totalled $160 000.

18 What is the percentage of overhead applied to the total cost of Job N75?

(A) 40%   Ⓐ

(B) 50%   Ⓑ

(C) 67%   Ⓒ

(D) 150%   Ⓓ

19 What is the total over/under-applied overhead for the period?

(A) $15 000 over-applied   Ⓐ

(B) $15 000 under-applied   Ⓑ

(C) $38 200 over-applied   Ⓒ

(D) $38 200 under-applied   Ⓓ

20 What is the gross profit percentage for Job N75 if it was sold for $280 000?

(A) 9%   Ⓐ

(B) 10%   Ⓑ

(C) 11%   Ⓒ

(D) 12%   Ⓓ

2.2.3 Process Costing

1 In process costing, if beginning inventory is not considered in calculating the total equivalent units, which method is being used?

(A) First In First Out   Ⓐ

(B) Last In First Out   Ⓑ

(C) Specific Identification   Ⓒ

(D) Weighted Average   Ⓓ

2 When the number of equivalent units is both less than the 'total units to account for' and the expected shortfall that usually occurs, this difference is called

(A) normal loss   Ⓐ

(B) abnormal loss   Ⓑ

(C) normal gain   Ⓒ

(D) abnormal gain.   Ⓓ

3 In the production report equivalent units consists of

(A) beginning WIP only   Ⓐ

(B) beginning WIP + units completed and transferred out   Ⓑ

(C) beginning WIP + units completed and transferred out + ending WIP   Ⓒ

(D) units completed and transferred out + ending WIP   Ⓓ

4 The number of units in beginning work-in-process were 4000 and were 20% complete with respect to conversion. The units started during the period were 8000 and the ending work-in-process inventory units were 3000 and 40% with respect to conversion. In the production report, what is the total number of equivalent units with respect to conversion cost, using FIFO?

(A) 9400   Ⓐ

(B) 9600   Ⓑ

(C) 10 000   Ⓒ

(D) 12 400   Ⓓ

The following information is relevant for <u>items **5–8**</u>.

Tortula Manufacturing supplied the following information:

Units in process 1 April 2019 (20% complete)	4000
Units started during April 2019	36 000
Units in process 30 April 2019 (40% complete)	6000

5 Under FIFO what is the total equivalent units?

(A) 33 200   Ⓐ

(B) 34 400   Ⓑ

(C) 35 600   Ⓒ

(D) 36 800   Ⓓ

6 Using weighted average what is the total equivalent units?

(A) 36 400   Ⓐ

(B) 36 800   Ⓑ

(C) 38 400   Ⓒ

(D) 40 000   Ⓓ

7 What are the total units to account for using FIFO?

(A) 33 200   Ⓐ

(B) 36 400   Ⓑ

(C) 38 400   Ⓒ

(D) 40 000   Ⓓ

8 What are the total units to account for using weighted average?

(A) 33 200   Ⓐ

(B) 36 400   Ⓑ

(C) 38 400   Ⓒ

(D) 40 000   Ⓓ

The following information is relevant for <u>items **9–11**</u>.

Penal Paper Products supplied the following information for March 2019 with respect to conversion cost.

Beginning work-in-process (20% complete)	4000 units
Units started during the period	6000 units
Ending work in process (30% complete)	2000 units

9 What is the total equivalent units using FIFO?

(A) 5400   Ⓐ

(B) 6200   Ⓑ

(C) 7800   Ⓒ

(D) 8600   Ⓓ

10 What is the total equivalent units using weighted average?

(A) 5400   Ⓐ

(B) 6200   Ⓑ

(C) 7800   Ⓒ

(D) 8600   Ⓓ

11 What is the total units Penal Paper Products have to account for under FIFO?

(A) 6200   Ⓐ

(B) 8600   Ⓑ

(C) 9400   Ⓒ

(D) 10 000   Ⓓ

12 To determine equivalent unit cost using FIFO divide

(A) beginning WIP by total equivalent units   Ⓐ

(B) cost added during the period by total equivalent units   Ⓑ

(C) total cost by total equivalent units   Ⓒ

(D) ending WIP cost by total equivalent units.   Ⓓ

13 Which business does not use process costing?

(A) Gas refinery   Ⓐ

(B) Ship building   Ⓑ

(C) Fish cannery   Ⓒ

(D) Chocolate manufacture   Ⓓ

14 Which business uses process costing?

(A) Specialty cakes   Ⓐ

(B) Taxi service   Ⓑ

(C) Property rental   Ⓒ

(D) Paper manufacturing   Ⓓ

15 The process costing system is different to the job costing system because

(A) Products are heterogeneous. Ⓐ

(B) It uses different manufacturing accounts. Ⓑ

(C) It provides a mechanism for computing unit cost. Ⓒ

(D) Cost is accumulated by department. Ⓓ

The following information is relevant for <u>items **16–20**</u>.

Sweet Tastes, a confectionery manufacturer in Grenada, supplied the following information for September 2016. The business uses FIFO in its process costing.

Work in process 1 September 2016	15 000 cases
Direct materials 70% complete	$33 000
Conversion cost 40% complete	$6750
Started during September 2016	150 000 cases
Cost incurred during September 2016	
Direct materials	$297 000
Conversion cost	$273 600
Work in process 30 September 2016	45 000 cases
Direct materials 60% complete	
Conversion 20% complete	

16 What is the total equivalent units with respect to direct materials?

(A) 127 500 Ⓐ

(B) 133 500 Ⓑ

(C) 136 500 Ⓒ

(D) 142 500 Ⓓ

17 What is the total equivalent with respect to conversion cost?

(A) 120 000 Ⓐ

(B) 123 000 Ⓑ

(C) 147 000 Ⓒ

(D) 150 000 Ⓓ

18 What is the total equivalent unit cost?

(A) $2.084   Ⓐ

(B) $2.176   Ⓑ

(C) $2.225   Ⓒ

(D) $2.329   Ⓓ

19 What is the equivalent unit cost for with respect to conversion cost?

(A) $4.00   Ⓐ

(B) $4.037   Ⓑ

(C) $4.40   Ⓒ

(D) $4.456   Ⓓ

20 How many beginning work-in-process units are accounted for with respect to direct materials?

(A) 4500   Ⓐ

(B) 6000   Ⓑ

(C) 10 500   Ⓒ

(D) 15 000   Ⓓ

2.2.4 Marginal Costing and Absorption Costing Techniques

1 Absorption costing is also referred to as

    I total costing

    II variable costing

    III full costing.

(A) I and II   Ⓐ

(B) I and III   Ⓑ

(C) II and III   Ⓒ

(D) I, II, and III   Ⓓ

2 Product cost for marginal costing differs from absorption costing because marginal costing does not include

(A) variable manufacturing overhead (A)

(B) fixed manufacturing overhead (B)

(C) direct labour (C)

(D) direct materials. (D)

3 The main difference between absorption costing and marginal costing is that absorption costing uses

(A) variable manufacturing cost in its product cost (A)

(B) variable manufacturing cost in its period cost (B)

(C) fixed manufacturing cost in its product cost (C)

(D) fixed manufacturing cost in its period cost. (D)

4 Absorption costing and marginal costing have similarities in that they both

(A) are prepared for internal use only (A)

(B) are prepared according to GAAP (B)

(C) use the conventional income statement (C)

(D) use direct cost as product costs. (D)

5 To find contribution margin using the conventional income statement

(A) expenses are deducted from gross profit (A)

(B) cost of sales is deducted from sales (B)

(C) total fixed cost is deducted from sales (C)

(D) total variable cost is deducted from sales. (D)

6 Operating profit (OP) under marginal costing is calculated by the formula

(A) OP = Sales – Total variable cost – Total fixed cost (A)

(B) OP = Sales – Cost of sales – Total fixed cost (B)

(C) OP = Sales – Cost of Sales – Expenses (C)

(D) OP = Sales – Contribution margin – Total fixed cost. (D)

7 Absorption costing product costs include

     I fixed manufacturing overhead

     II direct materials and direct labour

     III variable manufacturing overhead.

(A) I and II   Ⓐ

(B) I and III   Ⓑ

(C) II and III   Ⓒ

(D) I, II, and III   Ⓓ

The following information is relevant for <u>items **8–12**</u>.

Caldon Enterprises manufactures a single product and provided the following data for the month of April 2017.

Selling price		$120
Units produced	7500	
Unit sold	6800	
Variable unit cost		
Direct materials		$20
Direct Labour		$40
Variable manufacturing overhead		$8
Variable selling and administrative overhead		$6
Fixed cost		
Fixed manufacturing overhead		$150 000
Fixed selling and administrative overhead		$100 000

8 Using absorption costing what is the fixed manufacturing unit cost?

(A) $13.33 Ⓐ

(B) $14.71 Ⓑ

(C) $20.00 Ⓒ

(D) $22.06 Ⓓ

9 Using absorption costing what is the unit product cost?

(A) $74.00 Ⓐ

(B) $81.33 Ⓑ

(C) $82.71 Ⓒ

(D) $88.00 Ⓓ

10 Using variable costing what is the unit product cost?

(A) $68.00 Ⓐ

(B) $74.00 Ⓑ

(C) $88.00 Ⓒ

(D) $102.71 Ⓓ

11 What is the value of closing inventory under absorption costing?

(A) $47 600 Ⓐ

(B) $61 600 Ⓑ

(C) $71 897 Ⓒ

(D) $73 335 Ⓓ

12 What is the value of closing inventory under variable costing?

(A) $42 000 Ⓐ

(B) $47 600 Ⓑ

(C) $51 800 Ⓒ

(D) $61 600 Ⓓ

13 If there is no closing or opening inventory, then it can be concluded that

(A) The operating income of marginal costing is greater than the under absorption costing.   Ⓐ

(B) The operating income of marginal costing is less than the under absorption costing.   Ⓑ

(C) Cost of sales under marginal costing and absorption costing are equal.   Ⓒ

(D) The operating income of marginal costing and the under absorption costing are equal.   Ⓓ

14 The difference in marginal costing and absorption costing on operating profits is mainly due to

     I Opening inventories

     II Non-manufacturing overheads

     III Closing inventories.

(A) I and II   Ⓐ

(B) I and III   Ⓑ

(C) II and III   Ⓒ

(D) I, II, and III   Ⓓ

15 To determine the variable non-manufacturing overhead, which of the following are required?

     I Unit variable non-manufacturing cost

     II Number of units produced

     III Number of units sold

(A) I and II   Ⓐ

(B) I and III   Ⓑ

(C) II and III   Ⓒ

(D) I, II, and III   Ⓓ

1 The most appropriate system for recording service sector costing is

(A) Absorption costing (A)

(B) Marginal costing (B)

(C) Job costing (C)

(D) Process costing. (D)

2 Which is most likely not a characteristic of service sector businesses?

(A) Labour intensive (A)

(B) Capital intensive (B)

(C) Insignificant inventory (C)

(D) Perishable product (D)

3 Which is not a full list of service sector businesses?

(A) Banking, auditing, insurance (A)

(B) Beauty culture, hospitality, tour guides (B)

(C) Catering, car production, laundry (C)

(D) Education, legal, auto repairs (D)

4 Which words identify the nature of products in the service sector?

I Indivisibility

II Intangibility

III Heterogeneous

(A) I and II (A)

(B) I and III (B)

(C) II and III (C)

(D) I, II and III (D)

5 Which cost driver is appropriately matched with its business?

(A) Hotel – square footage (A)

(B) Hospital – Number of visitors (B)

(C) School – Students hours (C)

(D) Transport – Number of employees (D)

6 Which statement is true about service sector businesses?

(A) They have little or no inventory. (A)

(B) They do not need to determine cost. (B)

(C) They have a high direct materials cost. (C)

(D) They are highly capital intensive. (D)

The following information is relevant for items **7–10**.

Griffith, Sambrano and Cooper, an auditing firm, uses a job costing system and applies a predetermined overhead allocation rate based on auditor direct labour costs. The firm's budget for the year 2018 is as shown in Table 5.1.

Table 5.1

Audit hours	29 400
Auditor direct labour costs	$3 675 000
Support staff salaries	$1 923 750
Rent	$645 000
Other office expenses	$555 000

Alexander Caterers invited the auditing firm to bid for providing it with auditing services. The auditing firm anticipates that the job will require 360 audit hours.

7 What is the predetermined overhead absorption rate for the auditing firm?

(A) $0.524   (A)

(B) $0.85   (B)

(C) $53.125   (C)

(D) $62.50   (D)

8 What is the total overhead applied to the Alexander Caterers job?

(A) $11 451   (A)

(B) $18 593   (B)

(C) $38 250   (C)

(D) $45 000   (D)

9 What is the cost of the Alexander Caterers job?

(A) $33 337   (A)

(B) $56 843   (B)

(C) $83 250   (C)

(D) $90 000   (D)

10 If the auditing firm uses a mark-up of 20%, what is the bid price?

(A) $40 004   (A)

(B) $68 212   (B)

(C) $99 900   (C)

(D) $108 000   (D)

1 Which of the following benefit/purpose in budgeting will assist staff in achieving the goals and objectives of a firm?

(A) Communication ⒜

(B) Coordination ⒝

(C) Motivation ⒞

(D) Planning ⒟

2 Which of the following budgets starts the budgeting process in the master budget?

(A) Direct labour budget ⒜

(B) Cash budget ⒝

(C) Production budget ⒞

(D) Sales budget ⒟

3 A budget committee in a firm is made up of a group of key departmental managers. Their role is to

    I co-ordinate the preparation of budgets

    II review budgets

    III approve final budgets.

(A) I ⒜

(B) II ⒝

(C) I and II ⒞

(D) I, II and III ⒟

4 Budgetary control uses budgets

      I for planning and controlling a firm's activities

      II analysing differences between actual result and budgeted results

      III modifying and taking corrective actions to achieve targets.

(A) I   Ⓐ

(B) II   Ⓑ

(C) III   Ⓒ

(D) I, II and III   Ⓓ

5 Which of the following types of budgets are prepared by departmental managers?

(A) Self-imposed (Bottom to top or participative)   Ⓐ

(B) Negotiated   Ⓑ

(C) Imposed (Top to bottom)   Ⓒ

(D) Capital   Ⓓ

The following information is relevant for <u>item 7</u>.

Mc Sween prepares monthly budgets for the third quarter. He presented the following information:

- Sale of 120 units for July and 140 units for August. Management wants each month's ending inventory to be 60% of next month's sales.

- The finished goods inventory for the month of June consists of 50 units.

6 The budgeted total number of merchandise units to be purchased for the month of July is

(A) 84   Ⓐ

(B) 120   Ⓑ

(C) 154   Ⓒ

(D) 204.   Ⓓ

7 Which of the following is the correct format for a production budget?

(A) Budgeted sales in units – desired ending finished goods inventory units + beginning finished good in units   (A)

(B) Direct material purchased in unit + desired ending direct materials in units – beginning direct materials in units   (B)

(C) Direct materials purchased in units – direct ending materials in units + beginning direct materials in units   (C)

(D) Budgeted sales in units + desired ending finished goods in units – beginning finished goods in units   (D)

8 Which of the following schedules (or budgets) determine the payment pattern of customers?

(A) Selling and administrative budget   (A)

(B) Sales budget   (B)

(C) Schedule of cash disbursements   (C)

(D) Schedule of cash collections   (D)

9 A budget prepared for one level of sales volume is known as a

(A) Static budget   (A)

(B) Flexible budget   (B)

(C) Master budget   (C)

(D) Strategic budget.   (D)

The partial diagram in Figure 1.1 is relevant to <u>Item **10**</u>. It illustrates the steps of the budgeting process.

Figure 1.1

10 What is done at 'I'?

(A) Formation of budget committee   Ⓐ

(B) Preparation of initial budget   Ⓑ

(C) Revision and approval of budget   Ⓒ

(D) Preparation and implementation of budget   Ⓓ

11 Which of the following is the correct budget format for determining the direct materials budget?

(A) Production requirements (units) + desired ending inventory (units) – beginning inventory (units)   Ⓐ

(B) Production requirements (units) – desired ending inventory (units) – beginning inventory (units)   Ⓑ

(C) Production requirements (units) + desired ending inventory (units) + beginning inventory (units)   Ⓒ

(D) Production requirements (units) – desired ending inventory (units) + beginning inventory (units)   Ⓓ

12 A master budget is a set of

    I budgets made

    II forecasts made

    III schedules and budgeted financial statements.

(A) I   Ⓐ

(B) II   Ⓑ

(C) I and II   Ⓒ

(D) II and III   Ⓓ

The information below is relevant to <u>Items 13–14</u>.

Table 1.1 shows Gaynelle's budgeted sales in units for the next three months.

Table 1.1

Month	Units
January	50 000
February	60 000
March	80 000

Additional information:

- Selling price for one product = $20.00.

- Pattern for collections: 25% in the month sales are made and the remaining 75% in the following month.

- Accounts receivable of $600 000 for the last financial year will be collected in January.

13 The total budgeted sales for March is

(A) $600 000   Ⓐ

(B) $1 000 000   Ⓑ

(C) $1 200 000   Ⓒ

(D) $1 600 000.   Ⓓ

14 The cash collected for January is

(A) $600 000   Ⓐ

(B) $850 000   Ⓑ

(C) $1 050 000   Ⓒ

(D) $1 300 000.   Ⓓ

15 The cash receipts section of a cash budget may include estimated receipts such as

      I cash sales

      II cash payments

      III sales of investments.

(A) I   Ⓐ

(B) II   Ⓑ

(C) I and II   Ⓒ

(D) I and III   Ⓓ

16 Which of the following budgets rolls forward one month as the current month is completed?

(A) Continuous (Perpetual) budget   Ⓐ

(B) Zero based budget   Ⓑ

(C) Capital budget   Ⓒ

(D) Master budget   Ⓓ

The information below is relevant to <u>Item 17</u>.

A company presented the following information

Beginning cash balance	$25 000
Required ending balance	$10 000
Cash disbursements	$150 000
Cash collections	$90 000

17 The company must

(A) borrow $20 000   Ⓐ

(B) borrow $25 000   Ⓑ

(C) borrow $35 000   Ⓒ

(D) borrow $45 000.   Ⓓ

18 Which of the following is needed as a base to establish a sales budget for a company?

(A) Sales forecast   (A)

(B) Past financial statements   (B)

(C) Master budget   (C)

(D) Annual industry report   (D)

19 The benefits of budgeting include

    I the uncovering of potential bottlenecks before they occur

    II the uncovering of potential bottleneck after they occur

    III the provision of clear goals and objectives that serve as benchmarks.

(A) I   (A)

(B) II   (B)

(C) I and II   (C)

(D) I and III   (D)

20 Avery is planning to purchase inventory for resale costing $100 000 in July, $150 000 in August and $90 000 for September. The company pays 40% for the goods in the month of purchase and 60% in the month following the purchase. What is the budgeted cash disbursement for the purchase of inventory for the month of September?

(A) $90 000   (A)

(B) $100 000   (B)

(C) $126 000   (C)

(D) $150 000   (D)

1 Which of the following persons are responsible for setting standards for labour efficiency?

(A) Production manager and engineer   Ⓐ

(B) Human resource manager   Ⓑ

(C) Purchasing manager   Ⓒ

(D) Accountants   Ⓓ

2 A set of ideal standards

    I allow for no machine breakdown

    II allow for normal machine down time

    III allow for employee rest periods.

(A) I   Ⓐ

(B) II   Ⓑ

(C) III   Ⓒ

(D) I and III   Ⓓ

3 Which of the following is NOT used in the setting of direct materials quantity standards?

(A) Purchase price, net of discounts   Ⓐ

(B) Required materials   Ⓑ

(C) Allowance for waste   Ⓒ

(D) Allowance for storage   Ⓓ

4 The development of standards identifies

    I the types of materials to be used

    II the types of labour to be used

    III costs classified by cost behaviour.

(A) I   Ⓐ

(B) II   Ⓑ

(C) I and III   Ⓒ

(D) I, II and III   Ⓓ

The information below is relevant to <u>item **5**</u>.

Gysai Woods presented data for his company as at 30 April 2016 as shown in Table 2.1.

Table 2.1

Number of units produced	700
Number of actual direct labour hours	1600
Total actual direct labour cost	$15 000

The standard cost card indicates that 2.5 hours of direct labour time is allowed per unit at a rate of $10 per hour.

5 The labour rate variance is

(A) $8000 U   Ⓐ

(B) $1000 U   Ⓑ

(C) $8000 F   Ⓒ

(D) $1000 F.   Ⓓ

6 Flexible budget differs from a static budget because it is

     I geared toward all levels of activity with the relevant range

    II geared toward only one level of activity

   III static in nature.

(A) I   Ⓐ

(B) II   Ⓑ

(C) III   Ⓒ

(D) I and II   Ⓓ

7 Material price variances may arise for several reasons. The results of the variances may be

     I due to the quality of materials requested

    II due to the quantity and cash discounts available

   III because prices may rise faster than expected.

(A) I   Ⓐ

(B) II   Ⓑ

(C) I and II   Ⓒ

(D) I, II and III   Ⓓ

8 The formula for overhead controllable variance (spending variance) is

(A) actual overhead budget + overhead budget   Ⓐ

(B) overhead budget – overhead applied   Ⓑ

(C) overhead budget – overhead applied (based on standard hours allowed)   Ⓒ

(D) actual overhead expenses – overhead budget (based on standard hours allowed).   Ⓓ

9 The purpose of variance analysis is to provide information

    I of the difference between actual and standard performance

    II for management to improve operations

    III for management to utilise resources more effectively and reduce costs.

(A) I   Ⓐ

(B) II   Ⓑ

(C) I and III   Ⓒ

(D) I, II and III   Ⓓ

10 Which of the following documents tell management what is the predetermined manufactured cost for a single unit?

(A) Standard cost card   Ⓐ

(B) Job cost card   Ⓑ

(C) Process work sheet   Ⓒ

(D) Bill of materials   Ⓓ

11 The reasons for unfavourable labour efficiency are

    I poor training of workers

    II worker fatigue

    III faulty machinery or carelessness.

(A) I   Ⓐ

(B) II   Ⓑ

(C) I and II   Ⓒ

(D) II and III   Ⓓ

12 The reason/s for favourable fixed overhead volume variance is (are)

    I machine breakdowns

    II inefficient use of direct labour

    III fewer machine breakdowns.

(A) I   Ⓐ

(B) II   Ⓑ

(C) III   Ⓒ

(D) II and III   Ⓓ

13 Which of the following terms contributes to management planning and control in standard costing and budgeting?

(A) Predetermined costs   Ⓐ

(B) Actual costs   Ⓑ

(C) Cost allocation   Ⓒ

(D) Cost apportioned   Ⓓ

14 The advantages of standard costing are

    I Problems can be spotted on time and remedial actions is taken promptly.

    II There is difficulty in determining which variances are material or insignificant in amount.

    III It is useful in the setting of selling prices.

(A) I and II   Ⓐ

(B) I and III   Ⓑ

(C) II and III   Ⓒ

(D) I, II and III   Ⓓ

15 Which of the following sources of information reveal data such as types, quantity and price of direct material?

(A) Bill of materials   (A)

(B) Wages records   (B)

(C) Predetermined overhead absorption rate   (C)

(D) Variable overhead categories   (D)

16 Which of the following elements are used to determine the standard time per unit?

    I Allowances for breaks and personal needs

    II National Insurance (Social Security)

    III Allowance for rejects or spoilage

(A) I   (A)

(B) II   (B)

(C) I and II   (C)

(D) I and III   (D)

17 Fixed overhead variances focus on

    I input–output relations used in direct materials and direct labour

    II effective use of inputs

    III fringe benefits.

(A) I   (A)

(B) II   (B)

(C) I and II   (C)

(D) I and III   (D)

18 The purchasing of inferior materials may result in

      I favourable materials price variance

      II unfavourable labour efficiency variance

      III unfavourable materials price variance.

(A) I   Ⓐ

(B) II   Ⓑ

(C) I and II   Ⓒ

(D) II and III   Ⓓ

The information below is relevant to <u>Items **19–20**</u>.

During December, Sarah produced 5000 units of product. The standard cost card indicates the following for labour cost per unit of output:

- 2.5 hours @ $5.00 per hour = $12.50.

- During the month Sarah worked 13 000 hours.

19 The standard hours allowed for the month were

(A) 12 500   Ⓐ

(B) 15 000   Ⓑ

(C) 17 500   Ⓒ

(D) 20 000   Ⓓ

20 The labour efficiency variance for December is

(A) $500 F   Ⓐ

(B) $500 U   Ⓑ

(C) $2500 F   Ⓒ

(D) $2500 U   Ⓓ

The information below is relevant to Items **21–22**.

During December Ben produces 5000 units using 15 000 labour hours. The standard cost card indicates the following variable manufacturing overhead costs per unit of output:

- 2.5 labour hours @ $3.00 per hour = $7.50.

The actual variable overhead cost incurred was $30 000.

21 The variable overhead spending variance is

(A) $9000 U   Ⓐ

(B) $9000 F   Ⓑ

(C) $15 000 U   Ⓒ

(D) $15 000 F.   Ⓓ

22 The variable overhead efficiency variance is

(A) $56 250 F   Ⓐ

(B) $56 250 U   Ⓑ

(C) $7500 F   Ⓒ

(D) $7500 U.   Ⓓ

2.3.3 Cost Volume Profit

1 Fixed costs divided by contribution margin ratio yields the

(A) break even in dollars   Ⓐ

(B) break even in units   Ⓑ

(C) contribution margin in unit   Ⓒ

(D) contribution margin ratio.   Ⓓ

2 Cost volume profit (CVP) analysis studies the effects of changes in

    I costs

    II volume or levels of activity

    III operating profits.

(A) I   Ⓐ

(B) II   Ⓑ

(C) I and II   Ⓒ

(D) I, II and III   Ⓓ

The information below is relevant to <u>Item **3**</u>.

The figures in Table 3.1 are taken from Carlow's Income Statement.

Table 3.1

Net income	$10 000
Fixed costs	$80 000
Sales	$200 000
Contribution margin ratio	50%

3 The company's margin of safety in dollars is

(A) $10 000   Ⓐ

(B) $40 000   Ⓑ

(C) $80 000   Ⓒ

(D) $120 000.   Ⓓ

The information below is relevant to <u>Item **4**</u>.

Tex Inc. financial statements presented the data listed below.

    Selling price per unit $1000

    Variable cost per unit $700

    Total fixed costs $300 000

4 The break-even point in units is

(A) 176 units   Ⓐ

(B) 300 units   Ⓑ

(C) 429 units   Ⓒ

(D) 1000 units.   Ⓓ

The information below is relevant to <u>Item 5</u>.

Huey's records for the month of December are:

Variable cost in percentage form	70%
Target profit	$100 000
Fixed costs	$500 000

5 Huey's required sales for the month of December are

(A) $857 143   Ⓐ

(B) $1 333 333   Ⓑ

(C) $1 666 667   Ⓒ

(D) $2 000 000.   Ⓓ

The information shown in Figure 3.1 is relevant to <u>Items 6–9</u>.

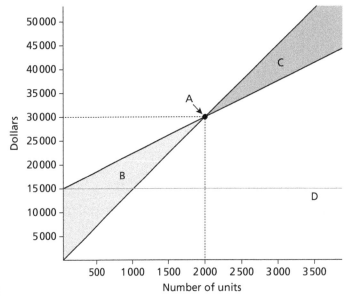

Figure 3.1

6 What does the point 'A' represent in Figure 3.1?

(A) Break-even point   (A)

(B) Fixed cost   (B)

(C) Profit area   (C)

(D) Loss area   (D)

7 What does the area 'B' represent in Figure 3.1?

(A) Break-even point   (A)

(B) Fixed cost   (B)

(C) Profit area   (C)

(D) Loss area   (D)

8 What does the area 'C' represent in Figure 3.1?

(A) Break-even point   (A)

(B) Fixed cost   (B)

(C) Profit area   (C)

(D) Loss area   (D)

9 What does the line 'D' represent in Figure 3.1?

(A) Break-even point   (A)

(B) Fixed cost   (B)

(C) Profit area   (C)

(D) Loss area   (D)

10 Which of the following techniques arithmetically determine values of fixed and variable elements in cost behaviour?

(A) Stepped down   (A)

(B) Repeated distribution   (B)

(C) Scatter graph   (C)

(D) High low   (D)

11 Cost Volume Analysis (CVP) assumptions are

    I fixed costs will remain constant

    II variable costs vary with activity

    III volume is the only factor that affects costs and revenues.

(**A**) I   Ⓐ

(**B**) II   Ⓑ

(**C**) I and II   Ⓒ

(**D**) I, II and III   Ⓓ

12 Margin of Safety (MoS)

    I is the amount that sales can drop before reaching the break-even point

    II provides a certain amount of 'cushion' from losses

    III provides an indication of risk.

(**A**) I   Ⓐ

(**B**) II   Ⓑ

(**C**) I and II   Ⓒ

(**D**) I, II and III   Ⓓ

13 Which of the following techniques is used to examine how the operating results of a firm will change when a predicted target is not achieved?

(**A**) Break-even analysis   Ⓐ

(**B**) Sensitivity analysis   Ⓑ

(**C**) Target operating income analysis   Ⓒ

(**D**) Performance analysis   Ⓓ

14 Calissa makes pencil cases for various non-governmental organisations (NGOs) to sell for fundraising activities. The cases are sold to the NGOs for $3 per box. The company's annual fixed cost is $100 000. Calissa intends to make an income of $25 000 by selling a total of 62 500 boxes of pencil cases. What is her variable cost per box?

(A) $1.00   Ⓐ

(B) $1.20   Ⓑ

(C) $1.80   Ⓒ

(D) $2.00   Ⓓ

15 Which of the following costs remain the same in total regardless of changes in the activity level?

(A) Opportunity cost   Ⓐ

(B) Mixed cost   Ⓑ

(C) Variable cost   Ⓒ

(D) Fixed cost   Ⓓ

The information below is relevant to <u>Item **16**</u>.

Sarah received a telephone bill showing the following charges.

Monthly rental of phone	$200
Cost of local calls @ $0.50 per call	$500
Cost of international calls @ $3.00 per call	$1500
Total bill	$2200

16 The cost of the bill will be classified as

(A) Variable cost   Ⓐ

(B) Fixed cost   Ⓑ

(C) Mixed cost   Ⓒ

(D) Step cost   Ⓓ

17 Break-even point will increase if there is a(an)

    I increase in total fixed cost

    II decrease in unit contribution margin

    III decrease in total fixed cost.

(A) I   Ⓐ

(B) II   Ⓑ

(C) I and II   Ⓒ

(D) I and III   Ⓓ

The information below is relevant to **Item 18**.

The following figures are taken from Drake's income statement:

Net Income	$50 000
Fixed costs	$100 000
Sales	$500 000
Contribution margin ratio	50%

18 Drake's margin of safety in percentage form is

(A) 20%   Ⓐ

(B) 40%   Ⓑ

(C) 50%   Ⓒ

(D) 60%   Ⓓ

The following information is relevant to <u>Items **19–20**</u>.

Fitzroy sells a single product. The selling price is $30.00 per unit and variable expenses is $18.00. The company's most recent income statement is given in Table 3.2.

Table 3.2

	$
Sales (5000 units)	150 000
Variable expenses	90 000
Contribution margin	60 000
Less fixed expenses	(30 000)
Net income	30 000

19 The contribution margin ratio is

(A) 20%

(B) 40%

(C) 60%

(D) 100%.

Ⓐ Ⓑ Ⓒ Ⓓ

20 The break-even point in dollar sales is

(A) $30 000

(B) $50 000

(C) $60 000

(D) $75 000.

Ⓐ Ⓑ Ⓒ Ⓓ

The information below is relevant to <u>Item 1</u>.

The following data relates to a company's decision on whether to purchase a machine

Cost	$200 000
Salvage value	$20 000
Annual after tax net income	$40 000
Method of depreciation	straight line

1 The machine's accounting rate of return is

(A) 16.7% Ⓐ

(B) 17% Ⓑ

(C) 36.4% Ⓒ

(D) 40%. Ⓓ

2 Cash outflows include

(A) incremental revenues Ⓐ

(B) initial (acquisition) investment Ⓑ

(C) release of working capital Ⓒ

(D) reduction in costs. Ⓓ

3 Two ways of assessing risks and uncertainty are

    I payback

    II sensitivity analysis

    III post audit.

(A) I Ⓐ

(B) II Ⓑ

(C) I and II Ⓒ

(D) II and III Ⓓ

4 Which of the following techniques centres on the time a project will take to pay for itself?

(A) Internal Rate of Return (IRR)   (A)

(B) Accounting Rate of Return (ARR)   (B)

(C) Payback   (C)

(D) Net Present Value (NPV)   (D)

5 The equation for calculating the initial investment of a project is

(A) cost of new project + installation cost – proceeds from sale or disposal of existing assets   (A)

(B) cost of new project – installation cost + proceeds from sale or disposal of existing assets   (B)

(C) cost of new project + installation cost + proceeds from sale or disposal of existing assets   (C)

(D) cost of new project – installation cost – proceeds from sale or disposal of existing assets.   (D)

6 Techniques considered as non-discounting methods are

    I Payback

    II Accounting Rate of Return (ARR)

    III Internal Rate of Return (IRR).

(A) I   (A)

(B) II   (B)

(C) I and II   (C)

(D) II and III   (D)

7 The time value of money depends on the

     I principal amount

     II number of periods

     III interest rate.

(A) I   Ⓐ

(B) II   Ⓑ

(C) I and II   Ⓒ

(D) I, II and III   Ⓓ

8 Which of the following techniques use accrual accounting figures?

(A) Internal Rate of Return (IRR)   Ⓐ

(B) Net Present Value (NPV)   Ⓑ

(C) Payback   Ⓒ

(D) Accounting Rate of Return (ARR)   Ⓓ

9 Capital investment determines

     I which specific investment a firm should accept

     II the total amount of revenue expenditure the firm should undertake

     III the total amount of capital expenditure the firm should undertake.

(A) I   Ⓐ

(B) II   Ⓑ

(C) I and II   Ⓒ

(D) I and III   Ⓓ

10 The payback method

     I considers the timing of cashflows

     II ignores the time value of money

     III chooses the project with the shortest payback period.

(A) I   (A)

(B) II   (B)

(C) III   (C)

(D) I, II and III   (D)

11 Which of the following would NOT be included in a net present value (NPV) analysis?

(A) Depreciation   (A)

(B) Salvage value   (B)

(C) Working capital   (C)

(D) Discount factor   (D)

12 The techniques which recognise cashflows over the whole life of the project are known as

     I Internal Rate of Return (IRR)

     II Net Present Value (NPV)

     III Accounting Rate of Return (ARR).

(A) I   (A)

(B) II   (B)

(C) I and II   (C)

(D) I, II and III   (D)

13 Which of the following appraisal techniques considers cashflows instead of accounting profits?

     I Payback

     II Accounting Rate of Return (ARR)

     III Net Present Value (NPV).

(A) I   Ⓐ

(B) II   Ⓑ

(C) I and II   Ⓒ

(D) I and III   Ⓓ

The information below is relevant to <u>Item **14**</u>.

Emma is considering a capital investment in a project. She presented the information shown in Table 4.1.

Table 4.1

Initial investment	$800 000
Residual value	$80 000
Expected useful life	10 years
Required rate of return	10%
Expected annual net cash inflows	$200 000

14 The payback is

(A) 2.5 years   Ⓐ

(B) 4 years   Ⓑ

(C) 4.4 years   Ⓒ

(D) 10 years.   Ⓓ

15 A stream of equal cash payments made in equal intervals is known as a(an)

(A) annuity   Ⓐ

(B) simple interest   Ⓑ

(C) compound interest   Ⓒ

(D) discount rate.   Ⓓ

The information below is relevant to <u>Item **16**</u>.

A firm with a cost of capital of 12% is considering a project with the cashflows shown in Table 4.2.

Table 4.2

0	1	2	3	4
− $5000	+ $2500	+ $2000	+ $2000	+ $1500

An extract of a table of the 12% discount rate is shown in Table 4.3.

Table 4.3

1	2	3	4
0.893	0.797	0.712	0.636

16 What is the net present value (NPV) of the project?

(A) $1204.50   Ⓐ

(B) $3896   Ⓑ

(C) $5000   Ⓒ

(D) $6204   Ⓓ

17 A project has an internal rate of return (IRR) of 12% and the cost of capital is 14%. At the cost of capital, the net present value (NPV) will be

(A) zero   Ⓐ

(B) negative   Ⓑ

(C) positive   Ⓒ

(D) equal to the internal rate of return (IRR).   Ⓓ

18 Cost of capital is synonymous to

      I activity rate

      II required rate of return

      III cut off rate.

(A) I   Ⓐ

(B) II   Ⓑ

(C) I and II   Ⓒ

(D) II and III   Ⓓ

19 Which of the following processes calculate interest on the principal and on all interest previously earned?

(A) Compound   Ⓐ

(B) Simple   Ⓑ

(C) Discount   Ⓒ

(D) Annuity   Ⓓ

The information in Figure 4.1 is relevant to <u>Item **20**</u>.

| Present value of future cash flows | → | capital investment | → | I |

Figure 4.1

20 What technique does 'I' represent in the above decision criteria diagram?

(A) Internal Rate of Return (IRR)   Ⓐ

(B) Accounting Rate of Return (ARR)   Ⓑ

(C) Net Present Value (NPV)   Ⓒ

(D) Payback   Ⓓ